Dancing Solo

Dancing Solo

FINDING YOUR OWN RHYTHM
IN A PERFORMANCE-DRIVEN WORLD

TIM M. GREEN

BEACON HILL PRESS
OF KANSAS CITY

ISBN 084-512-2219

Printed in the
United States of America

Cover Design: Brandon Hill

Library of Congress Cataloging-in-Publication Data

Green, Timothy Mark, 1961-
 Dancing solo : finding your own rhythm in a performance-driven world / Tim M. Green.
  p. cm.
  ISBN 0-8341-2221-9 (pbk.)
 1. Single people—Religious life. 2. Performance—Religious aspects—Christianity. I. Title.

 BV4596.S5G735 2006
 248.8'4—dc22

                                                        2006000140

10 9 8 7 6 5 4 3 2 1

Dedicated to my father,

O. Gerald Green,

who, in both life and death,
exemplified the beauty of God's gift of life.

CONTENTS

INTRODUCTION
TRAPPED IN THE RAT RACE

It was only a kids' game—just for fun, they said. But it felt like something huge was at stake as instructions blared through the megaphone, indoctrinating the squirrelly five- and six-year-olds in the rules of the game. "You've got to play hard, play tough, and play to win! It's every boy and every girl for themselves. There are no teams! If it's going to be, you have to make it happen!"

The kids soaked up the energy and broke out in thunderous applause. With all eyes looking toward the prized plastic golden trophy, the air was filled with aggressive excitement and competitive anticipation.

The game began! Some kids were natural athletes while others tripped, fell, and even suffered cuts and bruises. Some finished the course; others dropped out in a matter of minutes and ran to the sidelines to watch the more gifted kids finish the race. Many performed very well . . . just not well enough to win. Only one got the plastic trophy; another got the red ribbon and another got the yellow ribbon. A few were proud of their white Honorable Mention ribbons, but many knew what that ribbon really meant: "I tried . . . but I didn't *really* make it."

A SNAPSHOT OF LIFE

That cool October afternoon, filled with competition and achievement, was a glimpse of the life in which we all find ourselves from the first breath we take to the last one we draw before leaving this world. In between those two breaths a whole lot of living takes place.

With almost every heartbeat, we become increasingly absorbed in the never-ending cycle of seeking prizes, promotions, a parent's praise, a child's love, an employer's admiration, God's approval, victory over a dark past, or security in a bright future. We work to get more, perform to win, try harder to achieve, and hope that somewhere in all of those breaths we might place a plastic trophy or two on the shelf and hang a few colored ribbons on the wall.

We become performers in every compartment of our lives without realizing that it's happening. Each day, we are evaluated (by ourselves or others) in light of how much we accomplish and what we achieve.

This dilemma is only increased by the rapid advances in technology. With pagers attached to our sides, cell phones in our pockets, voice mails waiting for us at work and home, and e-mail piling up the minute we step away from our computers, we soon discover that we are on call 24/7. We take pride in always being available, ready to produce for *just* one more hour—even when there are no more hours left in the day.

This never-ending cycle of performing well and producing more is often magnified and complicated in the life of the single adult. To compensate for what might be perceived as something missing in an otherwise full life, the single adult can put life into overdrive with a busy schedule and overextended commitments. Squeezing just one more obligation into an already overloaded life demonstrates to family and friends or even to oneself that he or she is a significant contributor to the workplace, the community, or the church.

The young unmarried adult who completes a formal education or career training often gives everything *and more* to prove competency to colleagues while beginning a successful climb up the ladder.

The single parent becomes mom, dad, provider, nurse, cook, and chauffeur to children while showing the world that one person *really can* accomplish all the tasks of being a parent, friend, employee, citizen, and church member.

In order to occupy time that might otherwise be spent with a spouse, or prove that life is *moving on*, the single adult who loses a spouse through death or divorce can hide behind a busy schedule and overextended commitments.

This craziness even masquerades itself in Christian garb. Many Christian self-help books provide good, insightful help and ideas. But they can all too easily feed our performance-driven, accomplishment-oriented mind-set. We label the methods of our production-obsessed society with Christian principles, put a few biblical footnotes beside each suggestion, and call it the Christian way for success.

On the other hand, sometimes the daily ordinariness of life is seen as no more than an endurance test or a dress rehearsal for the real thing, as if the life we now have is some type of illusion or dream until the day arrives to *really* begin the life we're certain awaits us. We even apply a production-oriented mind-set to our walks with God, working hard to earn our payment in eternity. Similar to financial investments, we hope to *earn* dividends in the future through good hard work and a solidly performed life on earth. Unfortunately, we simply take the performance-driven mind-set of our society, dress it up in religious clothes, and call it Christianity.

THE HOPE FOR AN ALTERNATIVE

We all probably believe something exists on the horizon that, if acquired, would lead us to conclude, "Now, I've attained life!" For some, it's the completion of a degree; for others, it's landing a dream job, making money, finding a spouse, or retiring on a beach. Whatever it looks like, it's the point when we expect to feel satisfied and fulfilled.

The problem is that as soon as we arrive or achieve or attain, the fulfillment never really comes. Instead, we reassess our earnings so far and plot how much more (time, money, education, intimacy) it might take to pursue something greater and even more splendid. So we cash in our earnings and accomplishments and proceed to *spend* life on the next thing we are certain will fulfill our *real* desires.

Ironically, we can commit so much of our time and energy to *earning* life and *spending* life that we end up never *experiencing* life.

What if it's all a lie? What if life is something more than a series of disconnected achievements and accomplishments?

In the face of this performance-driven fantasy, there is an alternative vision that passionately announces to the human race: *Life is simply the good and pure gift of God!* As God's good gift, life cannot be earned or accomplished. It can only be given freely and then freely received! Life cannot be put off and experienced *someday* when everything is in sync. Rather, it is experienced, celebrated, breathed, lived—here and now—even when the pieces don't fit.

The biblical narrative expresses so many incredible ways of receiving and experiencing this free and pure gift of God. We hear the gift in the voice of the Creator who looks at the order and beauty of life and declares, *This is very good!* When chaos and destruction erupt, this same Creator does not shrink back and announce that life is defeated. Rather He declares, *Behold, I make all things new!* He continues to take the messy situations of life and create something beautiful.

We experience the gift of life celebrated in a community of people who labor diligently for six days but then dare to stop, take in a deep breath of free, unearned life, and bask in the beauty of God's good gift on the seventh day.

We see the sheer gift of life in the amazement of an elderly, barren woman who miraculously gives birth to a child. And it's in the joy of a nomadic, landless man who sets foot in his new homeland.

We participate in the celebration of the free gift of life in the clanging tambourines and dancing feet of a ragtag group of slaves who cross a mighty body of water into freedom. We taste this gift in divinely prepared meals of manna and quail for a hungry wilderness crowd, and of bread and fish for a multitude that is tired and hungry on a hillside. We hear it in the resounding *thump* of a mighty giant that falls to the tiny stone of a young shepherd boy.

This gift awakens as blind people blink their eyes to radiant light and run through the alleys seeing life in ways they never imagined. It is heard as deaf people who sat motionless throughout a lifetime begin dancing to the rhythm of the music. It is felt as untouchable lepers are caressed by warm, loving hands and their bleeding wounds are healed. It is smelled as dead, rotting bodies that lay cold in a tomb are animated with the breath of life and as bandages of hopelessness are peeled away to reveal brand-new skin of hope.

When all is said and done, we ultimately see this alternative vision of human life as the good, pure gift of God who wrapped himself up in fleshy, human skin and bones. As the Creator inhaled the first gasping breath of a newborn baby and exhaled the last gasping breath of death, He embraced the fullness of human life, from the womb to the grave! And in between those two breaths, the Giver of Life announces: *I have come so that you might have life . . . life to its fullest!*

A radically alternative understanding of what it means to be human emerges out of Scripture. In this understanding, life is not grounded in human productivity or based upon human achievement. It is not the payment for hard work or the reward for diligent efforts. Instead, it is simply the free and uncomplicated gift of God found in the very breath we now breathe.

In the midst of this busy rat race called life, we do not have to discover something new about life. We do not have to look for simple steps to cope with our performance-driven mentality. An alternative already exists. We can simply *rediscover* that this ancient biblical vision of life was available to us all along.

TWO VISIONS OF LIFE

Sitting in a restaurant the other day, I saw the vivid contrast between these two ways of experiencing life. A young man busily waited tables. He ran from one table to another, pouring water into empty glasses, bringing stacks of plates to hungry customers, clearing utensils from dirty tables, and quickly counting the coins and bills dropped for him on the table.

In that young man, I saw life as we so often know and experience it—a life consumed with working hard to get the tip, maybe even a promotion. A necessary tip—oh, yes! A necessary promotion—probably so! Yet in the busyness of working for the tip, he was deaf to the music and the laughter all around him, cold to the warmth of the summer sun that filtered through tinted windows, and blind to the people on every side of him.

My eyes shifted downward to a little girl sitting just in front of him. She wasn't more than five years old and was part of a larger group busily involved in a seemingly significant conversation. I imagined them talking about world affairs or church matters or perhaps resolving smaller issues like what dessert to order or where to shop after dinner.

Unseen by her family, the little girl climbed out of her seat and moved to the open space in the middle of the restaurant. At first, she raised her ear as if to catch a hint of music. She broke out in a smile, her brown eyes grew large, and she glistened as she looked around her!

Slowly, she began a childlike dance—swaying to the rhythm of the music playing in the background. Within a few moments, she began a cycle of three movements. First, she stretched her arms high toward the sky as if reaching for the stars, believing she could catch them. She then brought her arms close to her chest as if embracing and caressing one of her favorite dolls. Finally she stretched her arms straight out in front of her as if giving a treasured gift to everyone in the restaurant. In one smooth sweep, her outstretched arms went back up . . . reaching for more stars . . . collapsing toward her chest in an embrace . . . and then once again extending toward everyone in the room!

PARTICIPATING IN THE MUSIC OF LIFE

If only we could take a moment to stop and listen. In the midst of making tips, seeking promotions, and settling issues, the music of life is playing. It waits for us to join. It invites us to stop our busyness for a moment and listen through the noisy chatter of our hectic worlds. It challenges us to hear a new beat—the rhythm of life as a sheer gift, not a result of achievement. It even invites us to participate in the rhythm. Who knows? We may just climb out of the seats of our performance-driven identities and accomplishment-oriented lifestyles and discover ourselves breathing and moving to that rhythm—participating in the childlike dance of life.

With arms stretched heavenward and hands wide open, we *receive* this life as a sheer gift.

Having received the gift, our arms proceed to *embrace* that gift, truly experiencing life in all of its present beauty, simplicity, and joy.

Finally, with arms outstretched and hands wide open, we *release* life to all of those around us because no gift can remain a gift unless it is given away.

And now the cycle repeats because with our arms outstretched and hands wide open, we are once again in the posture to receive life as a gift. As we become like that naive, innocent child who breathlessly receives a treasure with wonder and awe, we just might come to understand what it means to receive life, embrace it, and release it as a gift to others!

Part One
THE RECEPTION—
RECEIVING LIFE AS A GIFT

Oblivious to the chatter and clutter all around her,
she climbed out of the oversized chair
and found a much more comfortable place
right in the middle of the wide-open restaurant floor.

After a brief but thoughtful pause,
she slowly began finding her place in the music
that everyone else was too busy to hear.

With her eyes shining bright as diamonds and her hands
    wide open,
she started the long, slow stretch as far toward the sky as
    she could reach
as if she had the optimism to capture the sun and the
    moon,
the stars and the clouds, the birds and the rainbows,
and every other good thing that she could imagine.

Reaching, reaching, reaching . . . caught!
And the celebration had begun . . .

1

The Simplest Gift

The phrase sounds so appealing: "Life is a sheer gift!" But this notion can all too easily be like a Sunday morning song that makes us feel good for a few minutes . . . until reality hits! When the warm, cozy feelings of Sunday worship meet the cold reality of Monday morning's alarm clock and we step out of bed to face the demands of the day, does believing that life is a gift really make any difference?

Our performance-driven world is always looking for one more easy way to achieve the good life. A few simple steps here and a list of helpful hints there might seem like the way to help us all reach the goal of experiencing life as a gift. But while that approach might benefit us for a few weeks or even a few months, steps and tips eventually grow old because our performance-driven appetite is never ultimately satisfied.

Experiencing life as a gift is not another way of *doing* life. It is a way of *seeing* life. Rather than beginning with a reformation of what we do, experiencing life as a gift starts with a *transformation* of how we think—a radical change in how we view living.

A RADICAL ALTERNATIVE

We are absorbed in a culture where the value of our lives is intricately related to how much we contribute to our society, families, workplaces, and even our churches. As long as we are growing and fruitful, we are deemed valuable. However, as soon as brokenness, frailty, or weakness emerges and our productivity decreases, our worth is devalued.

Our lives look a lot like the stock market sometimes. As productivity increases in our lives, our value rises. But as productivity decreases, our value falls. If we're not careful, the world tells us, we could even fall into human bankruptcy.

Is this really what it means to be human? Is the core of our human identity based upon the feats we accomplish during our relatively short lifetime? Are we only as good as our next production?

As the curtain rises on the biblical drama in the Book of Genesis, a radically alternative vision of the meaning and purpose of human life confronts and challenges our common performance-driven perception. Here we get a stunningly vivid picture of God's design for human life as a sheer and pure gift that can only be received and never achieved.

The story of our beginnings in Gen. 2 is one of deep intimacy. The life-giving, air-breathing Creator of the universe refuses to be aloof and stand at a distance from His creation. Instead, our God is the Potter who gets His hands dirty in the mud and water as He tenderly and intimately shapes His most prized artwork.

Having sculpted His perfect treasure, God proceeds in the most personal manner to breathe the very breath of life into this clay shell. As divine breath circulates through the empty earthen vessel, human life is animated: eyes open, nostrils flare, hands move, legs walk, a heart beats. This previously limp, lifeless piece of clay did absolutely nothing to achieve the breath that brought it to life. And yet, without accomplishing a single thing, it is fully alive.

This story is so much more than a sentimental childhood tale. It is profound; it is deep! Even more, it is mind-transforming as it paints a portrait of what it means for us to be human. It tells us who we are—here, now, today. The gracious and loving breath of God continues to animate, awaken, and enliven us. The breath we inhale is not a product of our own creative powers, intelligence, wealth, or personality. We can't manufacture it; we can't buy it; we can't earn it. It is a gift—a sheer, simple, and pure gift from a graciously loving God. Our capacity to inhale life is the result of our loving God's willingness to exhale it. *The very core of our identity is not what we produce but what we receive.*

The Divine Potter then becomes the Divine Gardener as He plants a luscious, tree-filled garden that provides not only life-sustaining nourishment for the body but also beauty for the eye to see and the ear to hear and the hand to feel and the tongue to taste and the nose to smell.

Imagine that! This God cares so deeply for the human life that He creates a garden that provides nourishment to sustain our bodies and beauty to enliven our senses. He provides all that is necessary to nurture us and bring moments of enjoyment and celebration. What a gift! We did not plant the garden; we only received it.

The Divine Gardener then invites us into a cooperative partnership with Him. We become the caretakers of His garden. God is incredibly vulnerable as He shares with us the care and protection of His creation. We are not passive observers of His good gift of creation; we are active participants and celebrants in it. We are integral members of this garden of life, not because we created it but because we are *given* it.

As beautiful as this gift is, God pauses and announces that there is something in His creation that is not appropriate. Up to this point, everything that God has created is pronounced as *good*—even *very good!* However, as He looks upon His human creation, He declares that it is just not fitting for the human being to experience this garden of life alone (Gen. 2:18).

God concludes that human beings must share life, intimacy, community, and fellowship with others who also laugh and cry and dream and hope and play and think and talk and imagine and love. This gift of life is designed for relationships. Human community becomes an integral part of the divine gift.

It's a sweeping contrast to viewing the source of life as human performance and achievement—breath freely given by an intimate Creator, a garden of nourishment and beauty, cooperative participation in what the Creator is doing, shared life in human community. It sounds too simple. It seems too childlike. However, God's counterintuitive vision of what it means for us to be human has far-reaching and life-impacting ramifications in even the smallest areas of our lives.

From the moment we step into the world, this life of breath and nourishment and partnership and community is a divine gift to unwrap and experience . . . *now*. What are we waiting for? Why do we keep it wrapped up and saved for tomorrow? It doesn't begin when we graduate, say "I do," climb to the top of the career ladder, move to the country, or cash in the 401(k). The breath is in us *now*. The garden of nourishment and beauty with all of its creatures surrounds us *now*. The opportunity to let our hearts and hands vulnerably melt into the hearts and hands of other warm bodies who laugh and dream and hope and cry is here . . . *now!*

According to the Giver, this gift of life is good—in fact, it is very good! Into our lives, this breath-breathing, garden-planting, partnership-sharing, community-forming God announces, *I give it to you . . . receive it, inhale it, eat it, rejoice in it, watch over it, play in it, share life in it. Take this gift of your humanity and be more than satisfied with it. Do more than cope with it. Live it! Breathe it! Celebrate it!*

TOO GOOD TO BE TRUE

We learn rather quickly in life to be skeptical of anything described as a free gift. As we mature, our adult cynicism adamantly states, "Nothing in life is free" or "If it sounds too good to be true, it probably is." We eventually stop asking, "Are there strings attached?" and instead ask, "Just how many strings are attached?"

In contrast to our awkward, adult way of receiving gifts, consider children. They instinctively know exactly what to do with a gift. They rarely scrutinize how beautifully the gift is wrapped or care how much the gift might have cost. With bright eyes of anticipation, they run to the gift and tear it open, even when an adult somewhere in the background is saying, "Save the ribbon!" They show their pleasure in a smile and exclamation of joy as they receive the gift and immediately try it on, play with it, or embrace it. In other words, they receive the gift as a gift and begin to *live it.*

The vision of life as a pure and simple gift seems like a fanciful, childish dream, and so we receive it like the seasoned, cynical adults that we are. The sheer joy of intimacy and partnership with God in what He is doing in His world disintegrates into a religion of legalistic performance in which we earn the grace of God through various acts of piety and service because, remember, nothing in life is free . . . not even the gift of life.

God is no longer viewed as the Gift-Giver but as the despot from whom we must hide out of fear. His creation is no longer received as a gift to experience but as an obstacle to overcome. The intimacy that we were created to experience with other human beings breaks down into relationships of competition and manipulation. Other people are no longer experienced as people with whom we mutually share this gift of life but as objects to use for our own benefit or obstacles to overcome and avoid.

Our inability to receive life as a gift goes back to the very beginning of the human story. Even though God announces that the garden of life is ours as a gift and that we are to take it, eat from it, live in it, see its beauty, taste its nourishment, experience its wonder, we say from the start, "This just sounds too good to be true." Nevertheless, God keeps saying, *I'm the Creator; you're the creature. I'm the Garden-Giver;*

you're the garden-receiver. Just trust Me. Let Me keep being the Life-Giver; you keep being the life-recipient. Trust Me!

In spite of God's tenacity to keep giving the gift of life, it seems that His alternative vision just can't penetrate into the way we think. Every now and then we get hold of a good suggestion or two on how we might more boldly embrace the gift of life. From time to time, we even resolve to rest in God for a while. But when we have to face realities of the world, we just can't quite believe it. We live like there is a catch.

Maybe we've been told so often that life really is what we can accomplish and produce that we become numb to any other option. Just like the first human beings, we keep eating from that one tree that promises we can be little gods of our lives—little creators, producers, achievers.

THE DILEMMA OF A FALSE IDENTITY

We are left with a huge dilemma! While at the very heart of our identity we are created and designed to be gift people, we end up with a false identity as performance people. As a result, we spend entire lifetimes absorbed in trying to discover who we are by what we accomplish and produce. One more incentive is always dangling just in front of us. We jump a little higher and achieve a little more so that *this time* we can really experience life to its fullest.

In the face of failure, some of us move or get nudged to the sidelines of life. We must conclude that we were never fully capable of living a *real* life. We take a position in the spectator stands and watch with regret, indifference, or defeat as others pass us by.

The strange delusion that the creation of life is somehow in our control continues, perhaps even extends, into a belief that we can also provide life to significant people around us. It can lead to being absorbed in working from our own power to sustain friends, aging parents, needy co-workers, and children. We draw a direct correlation between the significance of our own life and the happiness and well-being of others.

We are failing to realize just how utterly dependent we are upon a life-giving God to remain the Source of life to both ourselves and the people for whom we care. Our daily tasks are no longer carried out cooperatively with the Life-Giver. Instead, the joy of partnership with God becomes the dull task of merely surviving another day with God, with His creation, and with other people.

OUT OF PRODUCTION

There is a powerful alternative to living 24/7 as if life is something we can ultimately gain through our performance. Into our hectic, production-oriented lives steps the God who has been breathing the gift of life into us from the very beginning—even in those times when we are most strongly under the delusion that life is our own accomplishment. He refuses to stand by and let us live under this false impression. This God just won't settle for our mistaken belief. He is determined to be the life-giving, grace-bearing God in our lives.

God steps into our overdriven, performance-oriented lives just like He has always come throughout the story of humanity. He breaks into the lives of weak, frustrated, anxious, production-oriented people, and He promises that He will be the Life-Giver. He will loosen the grip of yesterday's brokenness. He will be present with us in all of today's needs. He will guide us into tomorrow's future. In all things, He holds out the promise of life as a pure, simple, gracious gift.

The Bible is filled with stories of this God who bursts forth with promise into the lives of women and men who come to the end of their capacity to produce life for themselves. To a generation whose hopes are crushed and whose dreams are demolished, He announces, "I know the plans I have for you. . . . They are plans for good and not for disaster, to give you a future and a hope" (Jer. 29:11, NLT).

To nomadic, landless families, God makes promises that they will settle in a land that flows with blessing and life.

To women who are barren, God makes promises that they will give birth to descendants who will eventually become as numerous as the stars in the sky.

To a runaway fugitive incapable of speaking publicly, God promises that he will lead a group of freed slaves.

To persons incapable of achieving and accomplishing, God makes promises that obstacles of great city walls will tumble down, that feared giants will be overcome, and that threatening enemies will be silenced.

Promises of hope continue in the life and ministry of Jesus as blind people receive sight, dead people are resuscitated, lepers become whole, sinners are brought back into the community, outcasts are accepted, and prisoners are released!

To a world that says only men with land can produce crops, only fertile women can produce children, only eloquently trained politicians can convince the power of the world to free slaves, and only physically elite warriors can carry out the battle, God declares an alternative and makes a promise. Those people who cannot produce or achieve or accomplish in their own strength receive sight, life, hope, and acceptance. The human delusion that life can be gained through what we accomplish is shown for what it really is through the vision of a God who comes with a promise to work in ways that we could never think or imagine.

The same God who set life into motion bursts forth into our empty, desolate, production-oriented lives with a word of hope as He makes a promise: *I will continue to pour out the gift of life to you. I will take the most barren, nonproductive places of your life, and I will act. I will take the most impoverished, desolate, empty places of your life, and I will work.*

CREATORS OF OUR OWN PROMISE

As God speaks of this incredible promise of life—a promise of a hope-filled tomorrow—we are prone to design for ourselves just how that "promised life" from God should appear. In certain seasons, we might decide the promise should take the form of acceptance to the right graduate school, alleviation of financial debts, a career on the fast track, or a position of influence in the church or community. When we decide we're ready, we might even feel the promise should orchestrate a lifelong, committed marriage with one whom we deeply love.

For some, we're banking on the fact that God's promise of life will mean freedom from the brokenness that we presently face. We design a future with no grief or tears, no fractured relationships, or no indecision about what we are to do.

When we begin taking matters into our hands and designing for ourselves what God's faithfulness should look like in any area of life, we place limitations on God. If those details do not work out the way we expected, then we conclude that either God was not true to what He promised or we failed to perform well enough to attain His promises—key phrase: *failed to attain.*

God leads us into a tomorrow that is filled with His faithfulness and love, but His plans for us go far deeper and greater than the tiniest details of life that we attempt to design and then footnote with God's approval. God's plan for us is wholeness—life that is experienced as a sheer and total gift.

RECEIVING THE GIFT OF LIFE

Life does not suddenly become a gift when all of the pieces fit together in one neat package. It's time to receive the gift wherever we are along the journey. Take it! Open it! Wear it, play with it, and delight in it!

The lifetime guarantee states that through good times and difficult ones, during routine and mundane days, when challenge and change are present, in seasons of peace and chapters of chaos, God is promising, *I gave you life and I will keep giving you life. Just trust Me.*

One thing is certain: this gift of life was never intended to be hidden away for safekeeping or simply used someday in the future. Unwrap it and experience it now!

2

Falling Back in Trust

He stood with his arms straight out to each side, eyes closed, knees locked. We had all seen the demonstration dozens of times and knew what was coming. But the participant's reaction is always so unpredictable that we watched with intrigue as if for the first time.

The speaker gave the instructions, "Now in just a moment, Bill, we're all going to count to three. And when we get to three, you're going to fall straight back." With a slight smirk on his face, he added, "And hopefully, I'll be there to catch you." Everybody, including Bill, laughed even though we expected (or at least we sure hoped) that the speaker would catch Bill.

Bill played the part really well. He took a few deep breaths and rubbed his hands together as if filled with anxiety.

The speaker held up his fingers and we all began the count. "One . . . Two . . ."

Then he stopped us. "Bill, are you sure you want to do this?" Bill nodded his head in agreement while we all laughed.

The count started again: "One . . . Two . . ." and then, after what seemed like an eternal pause, "Three!"

On three, Bill began falling back. But just at

the last second, he suddenly tensed up, bent his knees, and pushed himself back up.

Everybody laughed and applauded, as the speaker asked him, "Bill, don't you trust me?" Naturally, Bill's answer was what everyone expected: "Sure, it's just that . . . well . . . I thought I was going to fall!" The speaker looked intently at Bill and said, "Trust me, Bill. I promise that I'll catch you."

This time, Bill followed the instructions perfectly, and sure enough, the speaker caught him.

Throughout the afternoon, those words echoed in my mind. "Don't you trust me?" The scenario was about a whole lot more than an adult guy who was afraid the speaker might drop him. On one hand, it was a reflection of the human struggle to become fully vulnerable with other people. On the other hand, it represented the deeper challenge of surrendering our lives to a God who continues crying out, *Just trust Me with this gift of life that I am giving you!* Either way, fully trusting anything or anyone outside of ourselves is difficult.

OUR COMMON HUMAN STRUGGLE

Receiving the simple gift of life from God is a complicated matter. At times, this lesson is taught in affirming ways as we are given a significant responsibility and proceed to carry it out successfully. The highest compliment is paid to a young child when we ask, "Did you do that all by yourself?" Hearing words of affirmation like, "You did well," confirm that we really can make significant accomplishments on our own.

At other times, however, the lesson is taught with incredible anguish and heartbreaking pain as commitments and promises to us are broken. Over time, the cliché becomes a conviction: "You can't trust anybody but yourself."

No wonder our society is mesmerized by lone rangers who survive all alone on the island without being voted off. Allowing our lives to fall back into anybody's hands, including God's, becomes a near impossibility. It just makes us too vulnerable; we could too easily be dropped, disappointed, and even betrayed.

RESPONDING TO GRACE

Despite the challenge, God calls us to fall into His divine arms, receive life as a sheer gift, and discover the very core of our identity in the grace of God. If that's true, there is ultimately only one legitimate way to respond—we must fall back. It means knowing that if He doesn't catch us, we are hopeless. However, if He does, life takes on completely new dimensions and meaning.

This life-giving God holds out the same promise of grace that He held from the very beginning: *I give you this life as a sheer gift, and I promise that I will continue giving you this gift. Now just receive it, and . . . trust Me!*

The invitation to receive life as a gift by trusting God leaves us in an incredibly awkward position. After all the cords of dependence on others are finally cut and we celebrate the ability to stand on our own two feet, we hear of a life of dependence and trust in a God that we can't even see! Our dilemma is great. We are creatures—*receivers* of life —with a deep-seeded inclination for wanting to be something other than what and who we are. We would rather be creators—*producers*—of life. As a result of this ingrained tendency, we just can't trust grace . . . completely.

Oh, sure, many of us partially buy into the idea of grace— at least enough to sing "Amazing grace how sweet the sound / that saved a wretch like me." We accept the concept just enough to know that forgiveness of our sins and eternity in heaven is a theoretical gift from God. However, we struggle with all of the real-life living between now and heaven— missed promotions, conflict with people we love, busyness in our calendars, politics within the church, financial strain, and so forth. No wonder the concept of grace evaporates when it comes to making it through everyday matters.

Sometimes it seems helpful to compartmentalize so we divide our lives into the sacred/spiritual and the secular/commonplace. God's grace and our trust have more to do with the sacred part of our lives. Grace is what Jesus did to get us to heaven but has little or nothing to do with everyday living. Performance, accomplishment, and productivity have more to do with the secular side of our lives. In the commonplace, everyday arena of life, our motto remains: "If it's going to be, it really is up to me."

So our lives suffer an internal split. On one hand, we are grace people, trusting God's love and mercy, forgiveness, and life after death. On the other hand, we are performance-oriented people, trusting our own schemes and devices to help us survive and perhaps even succeed at real life.

Although we make nice, neat divisions between our spiritual and secular lives, God doesn't! He sees life in its entirety where all of the scattered, fragmented pieces—physical, intellectual, spiritual, relational—actually make one whole. In fact, the biblical notion of peace, or *shalom*, is just that—life that is whole and undivided.

As a result, as God invites us to fall back into his arms, He is not simply saying, *Trust Me with the part of your life that you call spiritual.* Rather, He is saying, *Trust Me with the entirety of your life; trust Me wholly, undividedly, completely.*

Trusting *fully* in another makes us vulnerable, and vulnerability is always tough—even with God. Vulnerability forces us to recognize and accept the fact that we can no longer manipulate the pieces, people, even the God of our lives, in order to finally find life. We come to the mind-changing realization that life truly is *given* to us, and we cannot perform well enough or work hard enough or produce enough or achieve enough to acquire life for ourselves. With arms straight out and knees locked, we fall back into the arms of the God who breathed life into us in the first place and who continues to promise, *I will keep breathing life into you . . . trust Me!*

Although the vulnerability factor is a common human

struggle, it is often a unique struggle for single adults. We learn over a period of time and through various circumstances that we must fend for ourselves. After all, if I don't cook my meal or at least stop and pick something up to eat, who will? If I don't clean the house, who will? If I don't pay the bills, who will? Unless I provide for and take care of myself, nobody else will.

This independence that we sometimes joyfully accept and other times resent can spill over into the larger view of life so that everything is seen as resting on our shoulders. It seems like so much depends on our performance and adequacy.

Becoming vulnerable enough to fall back into the arms of the life-giving God in *entire* trust is one of the greatest challenges we face—single or not. It requires acknowledging and accepting that life is not our own achievement, but it indeed is the good, free gift of God.

ECHOES FROM THE WILDERNESS

We aren't the first people to struggle with undivided trust in God. The challenge for the Israelites to trust during the 40 years that they lived (or we might even say, simply attempted to survive) in the wilderness is particularly fascinating.

The stories ring loud and clear in our own journeys today. We see ourselves; we see our own struggles to trust this gift-giving, life-breathing God.

The people of Israel grow hungry, and God feeds them with manna and quail (Exod. 16). They become thirsty, and God gives them gushing water (17:1-7). Their very existence is threatened by the pirate-like Amalekites, and God fights the battles (vv. 8-16).

Throughout these stories, their unrest, anxiety, performance-driven mind-set, and fear drive them to take matters into their own hands. However, God keeps traveling with them. When confronted with difficulties and dead ends, they engage in quarrels and dissensions, yet God remains tenaciously faithful.

We all know the wilderness seasons of life too well. They are the in between times—we remember the incredible days of yesterday when God parted a Red Sea in our lives, and we hope for a tomorrow when God will once again divide the waters of the Jordan and take us into a hope-filled future, a land that flows with milk and honey. But in between the deliverance days of yesterday and the hope-filled days of tomorrow, there's a lot of living that must happen.

The wilderness seasons of life always follow the stories of God's deliverance. Yesterday, God was faithful and did some amazing things. We were impressed enough to trust Him for a little while. But soon, the going gets tough. All we can see ahead of us is the wilderness; all we know is that our stomachs are growling with hunger and our throats are drying out from thirst. Threats from outside are beginning to invade our lives, and our pulse is moving to the rhythm of fear. Panic sets in as we see ourselves *going* nowhere. We feel stuck! We forget that we're on a journey, and we begin believing that the rest of life might be spent right out here in the middle of the dry, barren, dangerous wilderness.

In the middle of nowhere the looming question is, *Will God really be faithful?* That question takes on many forms: *Where is He?* or, *As messed up as the situation is, how can He be faithful?* or, *Does He even care?*

God continues to do faithfully what He has done all along: nourish, heal, fight the battles, and give guidance. However, in the wilderness, changed circumstances, uncertainty over what tomorrow will bring, and indecision over what to do today can cause us to suffer from amnesia, forgetting what God did in the past and losing sight of the God who is with us in the present, taking us into a hope-filled tomorrow.

Our ancestors' journey in the wilderness holds a mirror to our own lives. It seems we often experience the same wilderness syndromes that they did. Let's take a look at a few of these syndromes.

1. The Glorified Past Syndrome. Often, in the wilderness period, we conclude that today can never live up to yesterday. Living in the memories of the past, we remember the good old days, and we want to return. The memories of yesterday cast such a long shadow over today that all we can see and imagine is yesterday.

In the face of the uncertainties of the wilderness, our ancestors so glorified the time when they were slaves in Egypt that they began imagining it as something it wasn't. Sometimes we do the same. We decide that life was so much better back then—before we relocated, before we lost a dear friend, before the breakup of a relationship, before we got this job. If only things had not changed, then . . .

The Israelites eventually came to see that the God who was with them in the past was still with them in the present. Trusting this God meant knowing that the God who was faithful in the past would be faithful today and would faithfully journey with them into tomorrow.

2. The What If? Syndrome. As our ancestors saw the potential threats of the wilderness, the familiar what if questions were asked. Panic set in as they imagined the potential dangers awaiting them. *What if we die here; what if we can't survive here; what if this is the end; what if this is the way it's always going to be?*

The journey through the wilderness seasons of life often triggers a sense of panic that can seize our minds and paralyze our ability to move ahead. An imagined future made up of the many what ifs . . . leaves us lost in the fears of what might happen or what could take place if . . . Imaginations about the future can become so real that we begin acting on them and proceed as if they are reality.

God's invitation for us to fall back into His arms in complete trust is a challenge to move beyond the paralysis of what if and instead rest in knowing He will faithfully move us into tomorrow . . . even if the what if does occur in our lives. The fears of what if can be confronted face-to-face not because we can fight off the potential threats but because

the God who gives us this gift of life in the first place is dependable and trustworthy.

3. The Bah, Humbug! Syndrome. In the wilderness, things
can take on a negative complexion. Even the gifts of God
seem negative! Do you remember how our ancestors responded to the gift of manna? It was nothing short of a
daily miracle of provision and nourishment, but they still
found a reason to complain. They said something like this,
"We remember the fish we ate in Egypt at no cost—also the
cucumbers, melons, leeks, onions and garlic. But now we
have lost our appetite; we never see anything but this manna!" (Num. 11:5-6, NIV).

As we journey through the wilderness of life, it seems any
situation would be better than the current one. Anywhere
but here would be an improvement. In these times, the familiar phrase fits perfectly: *When it rains, it pours.* The pieces
of our fractured lives are so scattered that ever experiencing
wholeness again seems impossible.

Even in those seasons, when all of life becomes colored
by shades of negativity and pessimism, we are again invited
to fall back trustingly into the arms of the life-giving God.
He invites us to view life through lenses other than cynicism
and discontent. He calls us to trust Him even when we feel
like everything is going against us.

4. The I'll Do It on My Own Syndrome. Impatience was one
of the most common responses of our ancestors in the wilderness. As a result, they often got ahead of God.

Moses' own brother and sister, along with his assistants
and the community as a whole, felt they knew better than
God. When life just doesn't seem to move along as quickly as
we wish it would, we can easily make rash decisions without
thought and without prayer—just to get life moving again.

This wilderness reaction is really not anything new for
God's people. All the way back to the time of Abraham and
Sarah, we see a propensity to get ahead of God and act on
impulse. When they looked at their situation and saw nothing but impossible barrenness, they brought their maid, Ha-

gar, onto the stage of their lives (Gen. 16). They lost sight of the fact that God's promise was about showcasing His gracious activity, not human ability.

5. _The Golden Calf Syndrome._ After deciding they had waited at the bottom of Mount Sinai long enough, our ancestors finally decided to intervene. Rather than expecting God to act, they fixed the problem by creating a god they could touch and feel. The creatures became the creators of a golden calf they felt was more deserving of their worship than the God who was performing miracles all around them.

They wanted a God they could control. Sound familiar? Idol-making is always the result of our lack of trust. We probably aren't bowing down before golden calves or little clay statues, but the spiritual trap is the same: we want to define how and when God appears and works in our lives. No longer is our worship focused upon a God who graciously and freely gives us life. Our focus falls on keeping God under control and manipulating Him.

The problem is that when He works in our lives in a way that's different from the limits we placed on Him, we don't recognize it as God working.

6. _The There Are Giants over There Syndrome._ What a future God held for our ancestors! As the spies brought back a single cluster of grapes carried on a pole, they announced that the fertile land of promise flowed with milk and honey. But they also reported on the obstacles. "The land we explored will swallow up any who go to live there. All the people we saw were huge. We even saw giants there" (Num. 13:32-33, NLT).

The door to tomorrow was wide open, but the future remained only an unrealized dream for an entire generation of Israelites—all because of a fear of giants!

Sometimes it just takes a rumor of giants in the land to frighten and paralyze us from moving into God's promise of tomorrow. A giant can represent things like fear, uncertainty, and insecurity, opposition from other people, competition, or merely the unknown.

We're all familiar with Goliath, the other great giant story in the Old Testament, but David's experience ends so differently. Like all of life's "giant situations," Goliath comes onto the scene with frightening words of threat and intimidation. "Come to me, and I will give your flesh to the birds of the air and to the wild animals of the field" (1 Sam. 17:44).

The giants seem so big, so menacing, and so destructive. We could avoid them; we could run from them; we could cower and let them destroy us. But consider the response of a young boy with undivided trust in the God who promised more than the giant could threaten: "You come to me with sword and spear and javelin; but I come to you in the name of the LORD of hosts" (v. 45).

The giants in tomorrow's land of promise pale in comparison to the God who holds tomorrow wide open for His children.

LIFE BEYOND THE WILDERNESS

Into the midst of worry, a radical alternative to our anxiety-producing, performance-driven mind-set speaks boldly and clearly. This option echoes from the mountaintop on which Jesus preached a sermon down into the valleys of our lives: "I tell you, do not worry about your life, what you will eat or what you will drink, or about your body, what you will wear. Is not life more than food, and the body more than clothing. . . . Can any of you by worrying add a single hour to your span of life?" (Matt. 6:25, 27).

Our paralyzing, fear-producing anxiety is then countered by these words: "Indeed your heavenly Father knows that you need all these things" (v. 32).

Jesus' words are not about having a stiff upper lip in the midst of life's problems. Rather, His teaching is grounded in a call to trust God *completely*—to trust God *undividedly*. The words "Do not worry about your life" are preceded by this statement: "No one can serve two masters; for a slave will either hate the one and love the other, or be devoted to the one and despise the other. You cannot serve God and wealth" (v. 24).

This teaching of Jesus does not mean that we should not plan for the next day or week or year. An easy misunderstanding of Jesus' teaching comes in substituting the word "worry" with "plan" and then concluding that this teaching makes no sense whatsoever; who wouldn't at least plan for the future?

However, worrying is not the same as planning. Worry is the anxiety that comes from believing that life is ultimately up to us. It is what happens when nongods (in other words, human beings) attempt to be gods (in other words, something other than human). Although we know in our minds that we are ultimately *not* producing creators, we continue to act as if life is about our productive creativity.

In Paul's admonition to the Philippians, this same *worry* is contrasted with bringing the needs and concerns of our lives to God: "Do not worry about anything, but in everything by prayer and supplication with thanksgiving let your requests be made known to God." He concludes this admonition with the assurance that "the peace of God, which surpasses all understanding, will guard your hearts and your minds in Christ Jesus" (Phil. 4:6-7).

So from the mountain-perspective of Jesus, what does a life of trust look like as we live in the wilderness and even beyond the wilderness?

- While the past may be filled with God's blessing, we can move beyond the glory days into God's bright future. We can trust God that life moves beyond the past.
- While we certainly may face the what if questions in light of tomorrow's uncertainties, we can know that God moves with us into tomorrow and even if the what ifs come to fruition, God will faithfully lead us and protect us.
- When the scattered pieces of our lives are just not coming together, it may seem inviting to go ahead and take matters into our own hands. However, we do not have

to lag behind Him, nor do we have to run ahead of Him. He will faithfully walk beside us in the now of each moment.

- While God may have appeared in our lives in various ways in the past and we may be inclined to limit Him by locking Him into those ways, we can trust that in whatever way He works, He will be faithful.

- Even if giants are ahead, the God who has been faithful up to this point in the journey of our lives will remain faithful. We can look the giants in the eye, not because of our strength or abilities, but because of the faithfulness of God.

JUST TRUST ME: A LESSON FROM A FAMILIAR SONG

I often think about watching Bill prop himself back up just before the speaker caught him. How many times in the wilderness, and even beyond the wilderness, have we almost trusted God fully but then imagined that maybe He needed just a little bit of our help, so we buckled our knees and pulled ourselves back up onto our own two feet?

Particularly when we hear the *good news* that life is a sheer gift, we *almost* believe it, but at the moment we are ready to climb out of our seats and get onto the floor and dance to the rhythm of grace, we realize that maybe if we returned to the table and produced just a little more, we might get a bigger tip. So back up onto our two feet we stand, refusing to fall *completely, undividedly* into the arms of a God who gives us life as a pure and simple gift.

Even imagining this kind of trust—a complete, undivided trust that views all of life as a sheer gift from God, nothing earned, nothing achieved—seems impossible. It takes too much vulnerability—too much *faith* in something, someone, outside of *myself.*

Perhaps the most appropriate prayer we can pray is the prayer of the father who came to Jesus asking Him to heal his demonic son. This father trusted Jesus at least enough to come to Him to make his request: "I believe; help my unbelief!" (Mark 9:24).

The heartbeat of this prayer summarizes that familiar gospel song that speaks of the *sweetness* of trusting Jesus . . . of just taking Him at His word . . . of proving Him over and over again. After all this affirmation of trust in this life-giving God, the chorus concludes with these words: "Jesus, Jesus, precious Jesus, / Oh for grace to trust him more!"

3

Becoming the Recipient

As I opened up the envelope, two familiar words were embossed in bold blue letters on the little white card: "THANK YOU." I took the card out and read the note inside. It was kind and thoughtful with loving words of appreciation.

I had given something that always seems appreciated, but to be honest, in the middle of the busy Christmas season it was also a very easy gift to give: a gift certificate to the local mall. I convinced myself that in case the certificate didn't have much of a personal touch, waiting in line at the mall for an hour and a half just to get the certificate was a lot of self-sacrifice—I guess that was my *personal touch.*

As I read through the brief note, these words caught my attention: "I also want you to know what I purchased with the certificate that you gave me." Then the note proceeded to tell me about the trip to the mall and the several-hour shopping spree that resulted in the purchase of a gift.

I appreciated knowing that the certificate was put to good use. Certainly, gift certificates are meant to be spent on something, not framed and put up on the wall or tucked away in a family scrapbook. They are designed to trade in and use on the *real gift.*

Gift certificates or money are definitely treated differently than other gifts. For instance, if someone receives a shirt, he or she wears it. If someone receives an appliance, he or she plugs it in and uses it. If someone receives a DVD, he or she watches it. But, if someone receives a gift certificate, another step is required—he or she must cash it in for something; the recipient must set out to *spend* it.

LIFE—SPENT OR LIVED?

Oftentimes, when we talk about our lives we ask, "What are you spending your life doing?" or "How are you investing your life?" Like a gift certificate, we often treat the gift of life like it's something to be cashed in on everything from completing a degree to owning the best toys money can buy or even acquiring the respect and recognition of colleagues. In all these cases, life is not the gift itself but the means by which we can purchase a gift.

If life is ultimately a gift certificate, each day is filled with the busyness of discovering the endless bargains we might get in exchange for our gift certificate of life. We become performance-driven *earners* who are always working just a little harder so we can get a little more added to our gift card. We become far-sighted *spenders* who are always reaching for the next goal, the next deal, the next prize on which we can cash in our gift certificate. We see the long distance goals, we just can't see the life right in front of our eyes.

As earners and spenders, our lives end up becoming no more than the lives of *consumers*—working hard to earn a little more so that we can spend a little more in order to possess a little more. Life is a commodity that is earned through productivity and spent on goods and services, comforts and possessions that we consider worthy and valuable.

In those seasons of life when everything is falling into place and we have the energy and time to go on a spending spree, life is always good for something else. Our investments pay off with the acquisition of goals, degrees, relationships, riches, or jobs. It is like having a gift card with a balance that never runs out, so we keep spending.

On the other hand, when life is difficult, the pieces are not fitting together, and we just don't have the wherewithal to shop around and spend life on something else, our gift card seems to have a zero balance. Maybe our investments didn't pay off like we thought they would and we're left short of acquiring our true desires. We even speak in terms of having a life of little or no value. The gift card seems good for nothing.

The seasons when our gift card of life is carrying a deficit are even more challenging. When life is filled with more IOUs than our time and energy allow us to handle, we can lose the strength and courage to even try to dig our way out. It becomes tempting to settle for a drained, empty, bankrupt life.

Matters like age, life circumstances, physical situations, and job status determine just how valuable life is at any given point when it is viewed more in terms of a gift certificate to cash in for something else. In contrast, if life itself *is* the gift from God, we become a very different type of recipient. We become recipients who no longer ask, *How much is it worth?* and, *What can I spend it in on?* Rather, we receive the gift in its completeness. We take it, wear it, listen to it, plug it in, taste it, see it, smell it, feel it, and hear it! In other words, we *live* it. We experience life as life.

OPTIMISTIC LESSONS FROM A PESSIMIST

Nowhere in the Bible do we find these two opposing ways of receiving life more vividly portrayed than in the Book of Ecclesiastes. Granted, many people believe this book is by far the most pessimistic book in all of Scripture. Nowhere else can one find language like "Vanity of vanities! All is vanity" (1:2), or "All things are wearisome . . . What has been is what will be, and what has been done is what will be done; there is nothing new under the sun" (vv. 8-9).

At first glance, the writer of Ecclesiastes represents the type of person we all tend to avoid. His cup is always half empty; even when the sun is shining brightly, the clouds must be waiting on the horizon!

However, when we look closely at what he is saying, the pessimism is *not* about life itself. In fact, his pessimism is about a life that is received and simply spent on trying to get something else. In this matter, he is not so much a pessimist but an amazing, optimistic realist.

The writer of Ecclesiastes asks the age-old question that all of life's consumers ask: "What do people gain from all the toil at which they toil under the sun?" (v. 3). This vexing question resurfaces frequently throughout the Book of Ecclesiastes. It haunts his life.

Once we spend our lives doing, performing, achieving, and accomplishing, what do we *get out of it*? As we read his observations, we are aware that this person *spent* his life on a little bit of everything. Reaching high into the sky with both hands, he grabs for a little bit of this and a little bit of that—a little more wealth, a little more power, a little more stuff, a little more education, even a little more religion.

Finally, after a lifetime of busyness, he says, "Then I considered all that my hands had done and the toil I had spent in doing it, and again, all was vanity and a chasing after wind, and there was nothing to be gained under the sun" (2:11). It's as if he opens his hands and discovers nothing but air!

After a lifetime shopping spree—*spending* life like a gift certificate, he makes this amazing conclusion: "There is nothing better for mortals than to eat and drink, and find enjoyment in their toil" (v. 24). This verse is often paraphrased: "Eat, drink, and be merry, for tomorrow we may die." Culture often interprets this to mean something like, "Go gluttonize, get drunk, and party hard, because this may be the last chance you have."

In the first place, the word "eat" means what it says: *eat*. Take the gracious food with which you are blessed, receive it, and eat it. The word has nothing to do with gluttony or overeating or partying.

The word "drink" in this passage is equally straightforward. It means *drink*. It has no connotation whatsoever of drunkenness. For that matter, the word has nothing to do with festivity or parties. It simply means, take the gracious drink with which you are blessed, receive it, and drink it.

Finally, the writer concludes with the advice to *take joy in your toil.* For many of us, just hearing the word toil probably conjures up all types of thoughts, such as hard work and agonizing labor. However, this word is not attempting to convey such ideas. It means the daily, routine tasks of our lives, such as driving to work, stopping to pick up a loaf of bread on the way home, pulling through the ATM to make a $20 withdrawal, and cheering kids to victory at the soccer game. The writer of Ecclesiastes calls these ordinary, mundane tasks *toil.*

The act of rejoicing is much deeper and broader and life-giving than merely *enjoying.* Rejoicing involves finally giving up the never-ending search for better things in exchange for our daily tasks. It is discovering bursts of surprise in everything—even the most frustrating and sometimes just plain, boring tasks. In the home, at the workplace, in the community, or at church, it is living abundantly in those settings and rejoicing in the good gift of life found there.

Eat, drink, and rejoice in your toil . . . The statement is not one of partying hard until we drop. It is the recognition that life does not require a cosmetic makeover or a druglike fix in order to be *life.* God will open up a day filled with daily tasks—some that we anticipate, some that we dread, some that we enjoy, and some that we tolerate. But in them all, life should be discovered and lived.

A FESTIVAL SCROLL . . . AND A MOUNTAINTOP SERMON

At face value, the observations by the writer of Ecclesiastes seem cynical. However, if we can be honest about this gift of life, we might not discover a maddening cynicism but an authentic alternative to our task-oriented, goal-focused, production-driven days. Indeed, we often raise the question ourselves: What *profit* or *gain* do we get from all of the busy-ness of our lives? And then we are brought back to our senses as the delusion that we have been living under for most of our lives is shattered: Emptiness! Emptiness! It all ends up as air.

Early in the history of God's people, the scroll of Ecclesiastes was read publicly each year at the Feast of Tabernacles. This feast was one of the greatest annual celebrations.

The people dwelled in small booths or tents in the vineyards during the festival. As they gathered the grapes and olives for the fall harvest, they rejoiced in God's faithfulness and celebrated Him as their provider. This celebration was filled with great merriment and festivity; they listened to the music, discovered the rhythm, and participated in the dance of life.

However, the festival did more than celebrate the fruit harvest. It commemorated the time when the ancestors lived in the wilderness. It recalled the stories of God providing for every need in miraculous ways.

As they heard the admonition to "Eat . . . drink . . . rejoice . . . ," they remembered the lessons learned so vividly in the wilderness: Life is not about our production of bread and water; life is about God's gift of bread and water. Life is not about defending ourselves; life is about God's protection and guidance. Life is not achieved, produced, or accomplished; life is given graciously and freely.

It certainly comes by no accident that centuries later at this very festival that celebrated the gift-giving God of life, Jesus said these words: "Our ancestors ate the manna in the wilderness; as it is written, 'He gave them bread from heaven to eat' . . . I am the living bread that came down from heaven. Whoever eats of this bread will live forever; and the bread that I will give for the life of the world is my flesh" (John 6:31, 51).

In the middle of this teaching on the God who gives of His very life, Jesus announces: "Whoever comes to me will never be hungry, and whoever believes in me will never be thirsty" (John 6:35).

In His Sermon on the Mount, Jesus elaborates on the same themes of Ecclesiastes—eating, drinking, and toiling. As we have already seen, His message begins with the admonition: "Do not worry about your life, what you will eat or what you will drink, or about your body, what you will wear. Is not life more than food, and the body more than clothing?" (Matt. 6:25).

He announces that if God cares for the birds, then He will care even more for us. Then, pointing to the flowers in the field, He suggests that if these flowers that do not even *toil* are clothed so brilliantly, we shouldn't spend our lives worrying about what we will wear.

Rather than producing in life in order to *spend* life, there is an amazing alternative: First, seek the kingdom of God and right relationship within that Kingdom. What is this Kingdom? It is living in the arena of life where He is *God* and we are not. It is affirming that God provides and we receive. It is believing that life is a gift from God and not an achievement of our own doing.

In this Kingdom, all of these *other things* that we might otherwise attempt to produce are provided. No wonder Jesus says, "Can any of you by worrying add a single hour to your span of life . . . So do not worry about tomorrow, for tomorrow will bring worries of its own" (vv. 27, 34).

BECOMING RECIPIENTS OF THE GIFT OF LIFE

The Book of Ecclesiastes, the Feast of Tabernacles, and Jesus' message from the mountain say a lot to us about receiving the gift of life. It requires a moment-by-moment, breath-by-breath, day-by-day reception. Becoming true recipients of the gift will change us forever and mark us with characteristics of true life recipients.

Characteristic 1: We Receive Life Itself as the Gift. While there is much that we can do and experience, and even accomplish in our lifetimes, none of it ever provides life itself. The source of the gift of life is simply a loving, life-breathing, gracious God. It is not given to us as a means to some other end. It is not given to us as something to spend but as a gift to receive and experience.

If we continue giving away our lives to those around us but stop receiving the gift of life, we ultimately have nothing to give. Life-giving people are gracious because they are continual recipients of grace. We give our time and energy and lives to other people simply because we are continually receiving. We love because we are simultaneously receiving love.

Characteristic 2: We Receive Life in All of its Simplicity. Because life itself is the gift, we receive it simply *for* itself. It does not become a gift when it is loaded with all the extra bells and whistles. The gift of life does not *become* God's gift to us when everything is going according to plan. Life does not become a gift when all of our dreams come true or when we finally enter into a career that is satisfying, discover happiness and contentment in a marriage relationship, find the perfect church in which we can worship freely, move into the house on the lake, or accumulate a large savings and retire at an early age.

Too often, the gift of life is completely overlooked because we expect it to appear dressed up in gold and glitter. Sometimes life may not appear as beautiful as we expect. It may have uncertainty, hurt, and unfulfilled dreams. Nevertheless, it is still life. Life also may not be what it once was. Situations and circumstances might drastically change, and we long for the old life. Nevertheless, it is still life in all of its beautiful simplicity.

Perhaps the 18th-century Shaker song articulates this concept most clearly:

'Tis the gift to be simple, 'tis the gift to be free,
'Tis the gift to come down where we ought to be,

And when we find ourselves in the place just right,
'Twill be in the valley of love and delight.
When true simplicity is gained
To bow and to bend we shan't be ashamed,
To turn, turn, will be our delight
Till by turning, turning we come round right.

From time to time, we need to break through all of the excess and extras that accumulate around us and recognize that none of it ultimately makes life the gift of God.

Characteristic 3: We Receive the Gift of Life in the Present. Life is never on hold. It never ends because of yesterday's changes, nor does it begin when tomorrow's dreams come true. The gift of life is not something for which we wait to arrive. This God-given gift of life is *now, here, today*!

Because the gift of life is received here and now, life is more than simply coping; we do not simply hold on and wait for the situation in life to change or pass. Life is experienced *now*, and this life is for living. Becoming recipients of this gracious gift means inhaling the breath God pours into our lives and knowing that *this* breath is the good gift of life.

Characteristic 4: We Receive the Gift of Life with Honesty. Recipients do not pretend, ignore, or cover up. In receiving life with honesty and integrity, we can then begin journeying toward wholeness.

Where there is brokenness in our lives, we must see it honestly and name it. Where there are haunting memories of yesterday, we can face them openly and honestly and begin the journey toward healing. Where there are shortcomings and weaknesses in our lives, we can acknowledge them without shame and experience God's power made complete in our weakness. Where there are struggles or addictions in our lives, we can transparently experience grace. Where there are fears and anxieties over tomorrow, we can admit them and become loosened and freed from their paralyzing grip on our lives.

Receiving God's good gift of life means seeing it honestly

and continuing to affirm that this life, with all of its jagged edges and even broken pieces, is the good gift of God and that He is with us to transform, heal, and make whole.

A RECIPIENT'S ULTIMATE RESPONSE

One of the easiest ways to cheapen a gift is to receive it with an assumption that strings are attached. How readily we can dilute the indescribable gift of grace by immediately turning our response into one of performance.

The most appropriate response to a free gift of the magnitude of life is summed up in one word: *gratitude.* At its core, gratitude is a mind-set, a way of thinking. It is the breathless, almost childlike wonder that recognizes that the gift is not a reward for something we have done and it can never be repaid or earned. As we recognize the nature of this gift of life, all we can do is exhale with gratitude and with thanksgiving for something that is given so graciously.

But be careful. Our gratitude toward God can very easily evolve into a closely related word—*gratuity!* Sometimes our depth of gratitude ends up becoming a tip based upon how well God serves us, how well He waits on us and performs. We come to *expect* God to provide the basics of life. It can require Him throwing in a few extras to prompt us to express our gratitude—our gratuity—to God.

The greatest demonstration of gratitude for God's gift of life is to consciously begin living and experiencing it. It is choosing to climb out of the seat from which we passively dream of what life *should* be and stepping into the adventurous story of God's good gift of life. We pause long enough to discover the rhythm of this gift and then participate in the childlike dance. And there on the floor, as we discover the rhythm of the music, we join in.

Part Two
THE EMBRACE—
EXPERIENCING LIFE AS A GIFT

As if she had captured a hidden jewel,
Her face shone brightly; she was content . . .
The gift was hers!

Now she ever so slowly—but oh so purposefully—
Began closing her hands one finger at a time.
With the invisible gift safe inside . . .
She lowered her arms from the sky.

As if she had discovered her favorite toy doll,
She brought her tightly closed hands toward her chest
And with glistening eyes and a beaming smile,
She held her invisible—but oh so real—treasure
To her heart . . .
And she held it there in a gentle embrace.

Closely holding, gently clasping, quietly embracing . . .
*   experiencing the gift . . .*
The celebration continued . . .

4

Going on the Journey

Most of us have taken a vacation with kids fidgeting in the backseat of the car, asking every 10 minutes, "Are we there yet?" The more they ask, the more we can't wait to finish the trip and arrive at our destination. The journey feels longer with every whine. We become preoccupied with finding ways to kill time or divert their attention until the trip ends. Those vacations can be such a nightmare—traveling two days to stay somewhere for two nights and then turning around and doing it all over again to get back home.

Just like those kids in the backseat of the car, many grown-ups sit in the vehicle of life asking the same questions: "How much longer? When will we get there? When can we get out and do something?" We just can't wait to get where we're going.

But there is an alternative approach that views the journey as the very essence of life—the stops, the breaks, the pauses, the moments of joy and the moments of pain, the moments of anticipation and the moments of arrival, the times of gain and the times of loss.

OUR JOURNEYING HERITAGE

As Christians, we have an amazing history of ancestors who viewed life as a journey and not simply as a destination. In God's earliest call to Abraham in Gen. 12, the Lord simply said, *Go . . . and . . . I will show you.* The focus of God's call was not on arriving somewhere; it was on taking Abraham on a journey that would forever change his life—and the world, for that matter.

God didn't give Abraham a road map; otherwise he would have trusted the map instead of God. God didn't give him a picture of the final destination; otherwise he would have trusted the picture. God simply told Abraham to step out onto the highway of life and keep on stepping. He promised that as Abraham traveled this road, He would be with him all along the way.

From time to time on the journey, our sojourning ancestors arrived at locations and camped out for a while. Along the way, momentous events certainly occurred. In these times, they commemorated the experience and celebrated by building an altar—a memorial—to God's faithfulness. They feasted and sang and rejoiced! But as tempting as it was to settle down and create permanent homes, they were committed to a journey. They pulled up their tents, got back on the road, and kept going. They refused to settle down and arrive prematurely because the life to which they were called was a journey. In the end, life was *the entire journey*— the big, the little, the good, the bad, the joyful, the painful.

When we finally come to the end of Genesis, one expects God's people to finally arrive at a destination. All along, God promised land and numerous descendants. If this story was a best-selling novel, the family would have driven down permanent stakes as the narrator wraps things up with, "And having arrived at their final destination, everybody lived happily ever after." But the end of the story shows no evidence of permanent stakes and final destinations.

As the fourth generation son, Joseph, lies dying, he tells his brothers, "I am about to die; but God will come to you, and bring you up out of this land to the land that he swore to Abraham, to Isaac, and to Jacob" (Gen. 50:24). And then he has them promise that they will take his bones out of Egypt and into the land with them.

It's actually the perfect ending. Throughout this story, the plot is never about arriving somewhere. It is always about the next line, the next verse, the next page, or the next chapter to the story of life. Rather than focusing on finally arriving at some destination, the focus is upon the God who faithfully makes the journey with a journeying people. This God never says, *Have I got something/someone/somewhere good for you. Now, you just meet Me down the road and I'll give it to you.* From generation to generation, the faithful presence of this living, guiding, loving God was known in the journey moment-by-moment, day-by-day, year-by-year.

The Bible repeatedly recognizes that life is an ongoing journey with God rather an arrival point. Though Moses was called upon by God to take the Israelites out of Egypt and into the Promised Land, he only *glimpses* the Promised Land from a mountaintop and then dies without ever entering it. It sounds tragic until we realize that his life was about so much more than simply a destination; it was a journey that took him across the Red Sea and into the wilderness and on top of Mount Sinai and to the shores of the Jordan River.

In the ministry of Jesus, He called people to follow Him on the way. Before He ascended, Jesus called His journey-oriented followers to continue the adventure by reminding them, "I am with you always, to the very end" (Matt. 28:20, NIV).

Frankly, the Bible's view of life is best represented by the punctuation mark called an *ellipsis,* or better known to many of us, *dot, dot, dot.*

In my early years of teaching in the university setting, I was grading research papers one evening when I was captivated by a particular student's paper. It was outstanding. However, on page 15, about two-thirds of the way down, right in the middle of a sentence, the student stopped and ended his paper with a *dot, dot, dot.*

The next day, I called the student into my office and after complimenting his work, I asked why he had ended the paper in this way. He looked at me with an inquisitive look that was obviously sizing up just how naive a professor I was, and then with a look of certitude on his face, he responded, "Well, it was about 3:30 in the morning when I was finishing this paper and I was getting extremely tired. I knew that I had to be at a 7:30 class, and I really needed a couple hours of sleep."

Then with a serious, yet flattering look on his face, he exclaimed, "I thought to myself, Professor Green knows the rest of what I am trying to say. He can complete it in his mind. So you see, I ended it with an *ellipsis*—a *dot, dot, dot.* That means the paper is not over; there is more to be written; there is more to be said; to be continued; *dot, dot, dot!*"

Admittedly, the student deserved an A+ for creativity in his response! Years later, I often still hear the echo of his explanation: "There is more to be written; there is more to be said; to be continued; *dot, dot, dot!*"

How true this statement is for the faith expressed in Scripture. Whether in good times or bad times, seasons of prosperity or seasons of death and destruction, moments of joy or moments of sadness, there is always more to come, another chapter to be written, and another line to be added. There is always another step to take on this journey called life! After every pausing comma and every stopping period and every perplexing question mark, the biblical stories always continue with a *dot, dot, dot!* The story is never over; it is always to be continued.

IMPLICATIONS OF THE JOURNEY FOR OUR LIVES

The journey-oriented, ellipsis-like lives portrayed throughout the Bible recognize and accept diverse seasons. Yet they also know that in the midst of change, God is continuously present and faithful. Neither great victories nor painful defeats are ever the final word because of a faithful God who takes the events and situations and circumstances of our lives and shapes them creatively into newness and goodness.

In contrast, settlement-oriented living is either so absorbed in holding tightly to what we already have that we become paralyzed and unable to continue the journey, or it leaves us so consumed with a perfectly imagined tomorrow that present moments and today's realities are missed. In the process, the journey and the presence of God who faithfully makes the journey alongside us are missed altogether.

The journey-oriented life is more than a dusty part of our past. It has incredible implications for living the gift of life today. It provides a dynamic alternative to a static view of life that simply seeks to reach a comfortable destination and live happily ever after. It also refutes many of the fallacies we've come to believe and replaces them with powerful truths.

1. The Fallacy of Getting There and the Truth of Living Here. Settlement-oriented lives look toward an imaginary, fictitious moment when we will finally arrive at a desired there. This is not to say that journey-oriented lives do not dream dreams, make plans, or have hopes for tomorrow. In fact, journeying people clearly understand that life is always going somewhere and that decisions made along the path play a major role in the road to tomorrow.

However, journey-oriented people recognize that dreams and plans and hopes for tomorrow are not the stuff of which life is ultimately made. They recognize that while we dream and hope, life continues, and they understand how easy it is to become so caught up in anticipating what tomorrow may hold that the here and the now of life slip by unnoticed.

2. The Fallacy of the Road Map and the Truth of God's Journeying Presence. While we never quite describe God's will as a road map, we all too often treat it as a set of directions that God might give us if we pray, believe, and try hard enough. We imagine we will find directions on this map for at least the bigger decisions of our lives, such as where we should live, where we should work, whom we should marry, where we should raise a family, and so on. We act as though God is playing mind games with us to see if we really, *really* want His will in our lives. Maybe if we show God just how much we want His will, then He will finally reveal it to us.

All is fine and good until something happens—such as misreading the map or making a wrong turn. Or perhaps somebody steps into our path and blocks our way. Or maybe an unexpected crisis requires us to pull off the road and tend to the needs of others.

When the road map of God's will doesn't show us how to get back on the right road, we can end up concluding that God's will is ruined in our lives and our only choice is to settle for a second-, third-, or fourth-rate route for our lives.

However, in the journey-oriented life there is no such thing as God's road map. Never in the biblical stories does God give any of His followers a road map that shows them where to go straight, make a right turn, a left turn, and arrive where X marks the spot of His will. The problem is that if God's will were no more than a road map or a set of directions, we would end up trusting the map rather than Him. We would put our faith in our own ability to follow directions rather than His faithfulness to guide us moment-by-moment. Obstacles, roadblocks, and hindrances on the way could legitimately terminate His will and His work in our lives. But God's will is never that static.

In the journey-oriented life, God travels *with* us. We have something so much more alive and at work and mobile and present than a dead road map. We have the living, working, moving presence of God himself to guide us.

The result of experiencing God's will and work and presence is throughout our journey-filled lives, it is a peace or wholeness with God's gift of life that goes deeper and spreads much wider than our circumstances. *Circumstantial peace* can be heard in statements such as, "If only I worked for another company, married someone else, had better friends, lived across town, attended a different church, or if only that crisis didn't occur, *then* I could have peace in my life."

Settlement-oriented lives seek circumstantial peace;

when the circumstances are just right, then life will be whole and complete. However, journey-oriented lives know that life continues moving ahead, changing, and developing. Peace and wholeness in life come not from the perfect circumstances but from recognition that God is with us throughout the journey—whether on the highest mountaintops, the deepest valleys, or the flattest plains.

As important decisions arise in our lives, God does not need to drop a map with a big red X marking what we are to do or where we are to go. Lightning bolts and booming voices are not the common way that God gives direction to His people. Rather, that same faithful presence that has often gently and quietly led us up to the point of the decision continues to guide us and give us wisdom in the decisions that must be made.

Those of us who are perfectionists can use God's will in our lives as an excuse to procrastinate in making decisions and ultimately become paralyzed, refusing to go any further in the journey. God just does not taunt us with His will. If He has a direction that He desires for us to go, He will provide sources of guidance and wisdom. Obviously we should take care not to make rash and impulsive decisions without prayerfully and thoughtfully thinking through the matter. We should be honest with ourselves as to why we would make one decision over another. We should share in conversation and counsel with persons who are making the journey with us and who desire for God's kingdom to be lived out.

In the end, as we desire to follow God's guidance in our lives, the context within which all decisions should be made is not one of worry and apprehension but rather one of rest in our faithful and trustworthy God. The heartbeat of God's will for all of our lives goes much deeper than matters like education, career, and marriage. God's will for each of us is that we trust Him fully. When our lives are overcast with anxiety and worry concerning God's will, we should first come back to this heartbeat and hear Him say once again to us, "Calm down . . . relax . . . and trust me!"

3. The Fallacy of God's Second Best and the Truth of God's Best. Closely related to the mistaken notion of God's road map for our lives is the frequently accepted fallacy of God's second best. No doubt, negative consequences can, and do, occur in all of our lives whether as a result of decisions that we make or decisions made by others. Nevertheless, there is nowhere in Scripture that teaches the concept of God's second best or third best or fourth best. This idea is a completely nonbiblical notion and has had an incredibly wounding and detrimental effect on far too many people.

Sadly, many, many Christian people honestly believe that they are now living in God's *second-rate kingdom,* as if God has junkyards for the forgiven who err or who are touched by the errors of others. How offensive this idea is to the kingdom of God! Where God is present and active, there is not a second-rate kingdom and there are no second-rate citizens. God never does substandard work—where God is at work, He *always* does His best! Broken relationship, loss of job, failure in education, physical abuse, career setbacks, changes in marital status, bankruptcy, physical challenges— no situation, regardless of the cause, leads to second-class citizens in the kingdom of God. Either we are full citizens, or we are not citizens at all.

Because of the nonbiblical idea of God's second best, it is easy for people to climb into the far recesses of the bleachers and watch the first-class citizens continue to perform. However, only in a settlement-oriented mind-set are there classes of citizens. The alternative vision of life in the kingdom of God is journey-oriented.

4. The Fallacy of the End and the Truth of a New Chapter. Because life is a journey and journeys include many twists and turns, transitions and changes are inevitable. Sometimes these changes take place because an era of our lives is over: the safety of living at home gives way to living on our own, a business contract expires, or retirement arrives.

At other times, a change in the life of someone else directly impacts us: a close friend or family member is relocated geographically, a company is sold or closed, or a shared relationship of love is no longer mutual.

Still at other times, the nature of life itself brings these changes upon us: children grow up and leave home, independent parents become dependent, our bodies face physical challenges, or we experience the death of someone with whom we have shared life's most beautiful moments.

While we could easily spend a lifetime asking the questions of why a transition took place or who is responsible or regretting what we did or what we didn't do, we finally must simply recognize and accept the reality that, in the journey of life, changes and transitions happen. They are a reality of life.

Since life is an ongoing, unfolding journey, transitions in life are never the end. Particularly in those transitions that involve a great loss, life ahead of us can seem hopeless, unpromising, and even doubtful. But life transitions, including those great losses that indeed bring pain and grief and wounds, are not the end. Transition moments of life are the hinges that bring one chapter to a close but *always* open a new chapter. The most dreaded transitions and the most feared losses of life are always accompanied by the God who opens the door wide into tomorrow and who continues giving us life to live with purpose and hope and anticipation.

Beyond each transition point life goes on much like a stream. From time to time, we feel like holding on to a branch and refusing to float in that moving stream. Sometimes we even begin imagining that the current is going so swiftly, we might drown. However, no matter how deep the water gets, no matter how swiftly the current of life flows, no matter how high the waves of change and transition become, He will not let us drown.

Disappointments and even perceived failures can also cause us to stamp *the end* on our passions and dreams. I have come to refer to these disappointments as making a wrong exit on the highway of life.

In my early years as a youth pastor, I took a group of 20

teens on a thousand-mile, week-long mission trip. Traveling all day and night for more than 36 hours, we were on the outskirts of our destination. We pulled off on Exit 17, and then discovered that we actually should have taken Exit 15. So what did I do? Did I get up in front of those teens weeping and explain that since we took the wrong exit we were returning home in order to start the journey all over again? Or better yet, did I explain to them that since we had taken the wrong exit, we would never get on the bus and travel again? By no means! That would have been ridiculous. Sure, we had to do some maneuvering and turning around and going back up one-way streets, but the journey was not over. We had a trip to continue, and that is just what we did.

On this journey of life, people so often take the wrong exit and conclude, "Well, the journey is over." Certainly taking the wrong exit might make it very difficult to get back on the same road. We may have to try a different route; perhaps we will even have different stopping points. However, the journey is not over.

Even when we have gone down the wrong exit, there is no reason to pull off to the side of the road, turn off the engine, take the keys out of the ignition, and say "I quit!"

5. *The Fallacy of One Season and the Truth of Many Seasons.* As we embrace the totality of life as a continuous journey, we ultimately recognize and even celebrate that life is comprised of a full range of seasons. In the past, I have visited areas where the warm sun shines year round and the rain seldom falls. I often dream what it would be like to live in that year-round bliss. I've even playfully imagined how delightful it would be to bottle up the warmth and sunshine to use on cool, overcast days back home.

As nice as it sounds to have this type of perpetual climate outdoors, think how marvelous it would be to finally arrive at a permanent season in life where every day is filled with warm sunshine at the job, in significant relationships with family and friends, in community and church affairs, even in our own emotions and feelings about ourselves. At the least, if we could bottle up the pleasant seasons of life and pour them out when the dark clouds hang overhead and the cold rain begins, the birds would begin singing, and the sky would once again turn blue.

While settlement-oriented lives desire to finally reach that destination where the sun shines permanently and the cold rain never returns, the journey-oriented life recognizes that in the journey, seasons come and seasons go. There are seasons of anticipation and expectation and awe and amazement when new life and new beginnings are taking place. There are also seasons of joy and celebration and laughter and high spirits when every piece of life's puzzle seems to fit perfectly and we wish that everything would stay that way forever.

Then there are seasons of uncertainty, questions, pondering and mystery when tomorrow is very uncertain and all of the finely laid plans aren't working. Yes, there are also the seasons of scarcity and grief and sickness and death when the very life that we have celebrated so gleefully seems to be nothing more than a vapor that lasts for a moment and then is gone.

Seeking to preserve summer year-round or attempting to move quickly from deathly winter to the promising new life of spring, the settlement-oriented life cannot help but seek an answer as to why the season has changed so dramatically. Could it be that I am being paid back for something wrong that I have done? Could it be that God is trying to teach me a lesson? Could it be that I am not the focus of God's love in the same way other people are? Could it be that my past or the past of my family is catching up with me? Could it be that I am not praying enough, trying enough, doing enough? The could-it-be questions can go on and on, and no doubt could-it-be responses have been given for millennia to women and men as they journey through the seasons of life. Much like the so-called friends of Job attempted to respond to his season of suffering with a multitude of could-it-be answers, many of us have experienced these right-sounding but very empty answers. No could-it-be answer can ultimately be definitive; therefore, in order to continue the healthy journey of life we must move beyond the could-it-be game and accept the *totality* of life.

Embracing this journey of life means knowing that the God who gives us this gift of life has himself embraced the *wholeness* of life from a manger to a cross. And in between, He embraced every season of our human lives.

Perhaps the greatest announcement of God's embrace of the *totality* of life is expressed by the apostle Paul when he declares: "Death has been swallowed up in victory. Where, O death, is your victory? Where, O death, is your sting?" (1 Cor. 15:55, NIV). Paul is not saying that grief and pain and death will no longer take place in our lives. Nor is he saying that when the dark moments of life come then life has become nonlife for us. Rather he is saying that the great, feared enemies of humanity—death and pain and grief and separation—are a part of the life of God himself. Even the seasons of darkness are swallowed up into the love and the grace of God. The coldest and darkest seasons of our lives are not avoided by God, but because He has walked through and tasted those cold, dark seasons of life, they are swallowed up into the very being of God. No season of life—good or bad, full of joy or full of grief, wholeness or brokenness—can separate us from the love of God that we have seen in Christ Jesus!

5

Breathing in the Moments

I couldn't believe it. After traveling more than 300 miles, I was about a half hour from my destination. I looked out the same window through which I had looked for the past five hours and something happened. Suddenly, it was as if my eyes were opened for the first time!

I saw the red-winged blackbird sitting on the fence post at the side of the highway. Just behind it, beautiful deep green stalks just beginning to birth golden ears of corn stretched for miles and miles. Gentle hills rose on the horizon, dotted with grazing sheep that looked like scattered puffs of cotton. My eyes lifted a little higher, and the deep blue of the sky was like nothing I had seen before. Grayish-white clouds floated along with the gentle breeze.

My first thought was, *I wonder how long I've been traveling through all of this.* My next thought was, *How did I miss it? The windows were there all along!* My imagination reeled as I began to wonder just how much I missed on this trip. I had traveled for nearly half a day and for some reason had not seen a thing.

I recalled that for the first 50 miles or so my mind was totally caught up replaying a conversation that took place just before I left. I spent a good deal of time wondering if what I said was the right thing, and then I spent a good deal more time thinking through other things I could have said, as well as what I might say when I returned.

Then I remembered that for a small portion of the trip, I was preoccupied with following the directions to where I was going. In fact, I took a wrong turn earlier and spent a good half-hour following the directions backward just to return to the point where I made the wrong turn.

Then, for at least a couple of hours, I thought through what I needed to do when I arrived, preparing what I would say and how I would say it. In fact, by the time I arrived, I had pretty well planned out everything I needed to do first, second, and last. I had a well-rehearsed plan.

But in spite of all that preoccupied me, why didn't I see anything? The radio was on the whole time, but I hardly heard a song. I drank about half of the coffee I picked up 100 miles back, but the remainder was cold.

The great obstacles to breathing in and experiencing the gracious moments of life are found in our repeated rehearsals of yesterday, our sheer busyness of today, and our anticipation of tomorrow. Pausing long enough to breathe in the present moment and inhale it as the gracious gift from God allows us to embrace God's good gift of life. It finds the rhythm of God in the cacophony of our hurried lives and busy schedules and perhaps even calls us to participate in the dance of life.

PREOCCUPATION WITH YESTERDAY

Who we are today is shaped by people, events, and circumstances that have brought us to the present moment. Denying the impact and influence of situations of the past ignores the reality that life is indeed a journey, and where we are today is the result of the road we traveled to get here. The refusal to face the past honestly can keep us locked in the past and even paralyze us from moving on into the future. We should see the past honestly, acknowledge it, and make it our own.

Yesterday most certainly provides a backdrop for our lives. However, yesterday is just that—a backdrop. It is not the stage on which we are living our lives. We can become so preoccupied with yesterday's circumstances and its impact upon our lives that we turn the backdrop into the stage itself. As a result, we end up living in a past that has truly passed and missing the God-given moments of today.

Sometimes we can glorify a certain event or situation so that this past circumstance is held up as a measuring rod to every occurrence in the present. With this glorified measurement, nothing in the present can quite compare. It may be a previous relationship or job or location or worship community. It may be a season when circumstances were so much more pleasant and filled with joy. As a result, relationships, events, opportunities, or even just passing moments in the present, come and go without ever being experienced as the good gifts from God that they are. The glorified past blinds us to the good gift of life that God is giving us *today*.

At other times, the past is filled with wounds and hurt. The pain of yesterday may emerge out of the guilt of something we said or did. It may come from a sense of regret that we did not do more or become proactive to remedy a situation. On the other hand, this pain that continues to survive from yesterday may be the result of what other people or institutions did or said that directly or indirectly affected us. Perhaps a person with whom we became vulnerable and in whom we put great trust let us down, or an institution for which we had great respect and admiration did not live up to our expectations.

As the painful shadow of yesterday is cast over today, we can easily be blinded to the good gift of life *today* and deafened to the rhythm that continues to play.

Certainly, before we can move on, we are in great need of making peace with the past. Making peace with yesterday does not mean that yesterday's memories are suddenly erased. Nor does making peace with the past mean that we shrug our shoulders and keep a stiff upper lip and pretend that nothing occurred. Peace with the past sees it as it was, but it also sees the past for what it is—the past. Yesterday is *yesterday;* it is not today nor is it tomorrow. Making peace with the past is recognizing that yesterday's air is stuffy and suffocating and then choosing to breathe today's fresh, life-giving air.

PREOCCUPATION WITH THE BUSY TASKS OF TODAY

It comes as no surprise that one of the greatest obstacles to experiencing the gracious moments of life is the sheer busyness of life itself. Our minds are so task-oriented and purpose-driven that we become focused on getting done what must get done. There's a job to do, a relationship to build, a salary to make, and a goal to reach. Today becomes the highway our lives take to reach the goals that must be completed by day's end. There is a great danger in traveling the highway of today, reaching today's goals, but never breathing in, experiencing, receiving, and embracing today. The gift of today becomes a means to a greater end—accomplishing our goals. Today is a gift, in itself, from God.

There is a remarkable story in the life of Jesus about two sisters found in Luke 10:38-42. Martha, the entertainer, was busily at work in her home, preoccupied with her many tasks, probably tasks that were dedicated to providing hospitality to Jesus, her houseguest.

Then there was her sister, Mary. She was simply taking advantage of the precious moments with Jesus as He visited her home. She sat at His feet and listened to Him while Martha kept grinding away at her tasks.

I've always been fascinated by Martha's words to Jesus: "Lord, do you not care that my sister has left me to do all the work by myself?" (v. 40). But I'm even more intrigued by

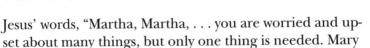

Jesus' words, "Martha, Martha, . . . you are worried and up-set about many things, but only one thing is needed. Mary has chosen what is better" (vv. 41-42, NIV).

Have you ever seen a Martha? Or better yet, have you ever been one? We can become so preoccupied even with good things that we miss the better thing. We become so task-driven that we miss why we're doing the task in the first place. We get so caught up cooking the meal to entertain our guests that we miss having a conversation with them. We become so preoccupied with being the perfect parent to our child that we miss out simply cherishing that very child. We can even become so preoccupied with living the good, devoted life for God that we miss out experiencing Him.

It's true . . . life is busy. But it is also true that the busy-ness of life is not the totality of life. The purpose of God's good gift of life is not to occupy us with 12 or 14 or 16 hours of busyness. Life is more than simply making it through to the end of another day. In the middle of the busyness, something else is occurring; it's called life . . . filled with moments, some small, some grand, some long-lasting, some merely fleeting. Do we see them? Hear them? Inhale them? Touch them? Do we even notice them?

PREOCCUPATION WITH TOMORROW

In the same way that the past certainly has a significant influence upon our present, the present has a direct effect upon our future. In other words, what we do today will have consequences upon tomorrow. Therefore, we make plans, we dream dreams, and we hope and envision the future.

Nevertheless, because we are so profoundly aware of the relationship between what we do today and where we end up tomorrow, we can end up spending the present in its en-tirety simply planning for tomorrow and never taking in the gift of life *today*. Even when the plans of tomorrow finally materialize, we will likely use tomorrow to make more plans for tomorrow's tomorrow.

It's very easy to get caught up in this cycle and become absorbed into the future in such a way that we find ourselves living in a realm that does not yet even exist. By always anticipating the what ifs and maybes, we can fail to experience the gracious moments of today. It can get so out of hand that we even begin living the moments of the present for the benefit of tomorrow's memories.

I will never forget my first breathtaking view of the Alaskan mountains. It was exhilarating! I reached for my camera and began to think how I wanted to take plenty of pictures so that I could show the beauty to others and look back at the pictures in the future. I had to take the pictures quickly, because the group I was with was moving on.

For the next five minutes, I took pictures from every angle, but when it came time to go, a startling thought hit me. I was taking pictures so that I could remember the beauty in the future. But ironically, I was so caught up in thinking of ways to capture memories for the future that I did not breathe in the fresh air of the moment and let the brilliant colors and captivating sounds soak into my inner being.

At the foot of the Alaskan mountains, I realized that the moments of today are not meant to be captured for the future so that someday I can live in the past. The present moment is itself the gift from God! This moment is not meant to be preserved and framed for the future. Tomorrow's sweetest memories are discovered in truly taking in, experiencing, inhaling the moments of today!

Oftentimes, the present is viewed like a line of planes circling the sky just waiting to land. We feel that we are in the holding pattern—anticipating the moment when we will finally arrive.

Our cultural ethos particularly feeds this mind-set for the single adult until we can claim the completion of a degree, the promotion to a higher professional level, marriage, or having worked through the final stages of grief in the loss of a spouse.

But the truth is that while we are circling the sky waiting

for our moment, life continues without ever being placed on hold.

I remember once speaking at a family camp. One afternoon, the teenagers had a scavenger hunt with a list of 20 or 30 items to find or accomplish. Among the tasks on their list, they had me write down my favorite Bible verse. Because none of them knew the cabin in which I was staying, I decided to make it a little easier on them and sit out on the front porch.

Another item in their search was located at the far end of the dead-end street next to my cabin. As I sat on the porch, literally dozens of focused teens passed right by and never noticed me. A couple of them even looked over at me, said hello, and kept walking straight ahead to the goal at the end of the street.

I guess I shouldn't have been that surprised. Isn't the scavenger hunt of our lives just the same? We have our list of a few dozen goals in life; the agenda is set. We are determined to reach tomorrow's deadline or next week's goals. With our attention given to where we are going and our focus set on getting there as quickly as possible, we often fail to look over to the side and see just what or who might be sitting on the front porch. Imagine what we might be missing. Oh, it may seem small and quite insignificant, but it is the multitude of small and even trivial moments that stitch together and make an incredibly beautiful and intricate quilt of life.

At other moments of our journeys, our stance toward tomorrow may be more one of dread or doubt. Perhaps the only certainty about tomorrow is that it will be filled with impossibilities and hopelessness. In other situations, we are not so certain what tomorrow will bring, but we have so imagined what it *might* bring that all we can see and think of are the maybes and what ifs. Concluding that we just can't make it through the maze of obstacles, we simply stand where we are, refusing to move any further in the journey of life. With our vision fixed on the impossibilities of an imagined tomorrow, we are blind to today.

Some who struggle with perfectionism face a similar dilemma when it comes to experiencing the moments of today. Willing only to act when we know we can act without error, we put off today what we think we can do a better job of tomorrow. However, as we all too easily learn, the tomorrow in which we can finally perform perfectly never arrives. Therefore, we spend a significant portion of today's journey simply procrastinating, finding other little things with which to busy ourselves. We ultimately cannot experience the steps of *today* that will actually take us into the journey toward tomorrow.

LIVING INTENTIONALLY

Finding the rhythm of life's moments begins with living intentionally *now*. In other words, we recognize that wherever we are, and in whatever situation we find ourselves, life is *now*, and we refuse to put off living.

As discussed earlier, it is especially easy for the single adults to regard periods of time as transitions, phases of merely passing through. We do not take the present moments as seriously because we are convinced that we are in a getting ready period for when we're certain that life will really kick in. So for today, we are preparing for graduate school, longing for marriage, pursuing a management position, or saving for a house.

The single adult who has been married and lost a spouse through divorce or death knows all too well that the period following loss can be viewed by the individual, as well as by friends and family members, as a transition time until a new spouse is found or at least until the feelings of loss subside. The person who does not plan to remarry following the loss of a spouse may believe the good years of life are in the past and somehow the quality and fullness of life today is second-rate. It certainly doesn't feel like a gift to cherish.

Single or not, living life intentionally slows us down long enough in the present to realize that we are actually experiencing life . . . in this perfect, sacred, spacious moment. Living intentionally recognizes that life is not a passive exercise. Life is not meant to happen accidentally. It is purposeful and deliberate. Life is a not a spectator sport; it requires our participation.

When dealing with the past, intentional living chooses to make peace. Those who live intentionally extend forgiveness where brokenness exists and conversations have been absent for years. The present becomes the crucial time to initiate healing, and if possible, reconciliation.

Intentional living also requires honesty with loss and the accompanying grief. It opens us up to recognizing glimpses of joy in the midst of sorrow in our lives. I clearly recall the days following the death of my father. At first, I had a strange sense of guilt when I wanted to laugh at something funny or find enjoyment with friends and family. I would say to myself, *I can't laugh; I'm supposed to be grieving right now.* However, I soon recognized that even in the face of the loss, there was a great gift in the very continuation of life.

God's good gift of life absolutely includes funny incidents, enjoyment, and persons to embrace and love. And in the midst of the most painful and grief-filled seasons of life, God's good gift of life remains filled with humor, love, intimacy, tenderness, and enjoyment. The only requirement is that we remain engaged in the moments.

Additionally, some of the biggest enemies to living on purpose today are those pesky if onlys and maybes. We don't have yesterday and we don't have tomorrow; we only have today, so we should really eliminate those phrases from our vocabularies. The best counterattack is to live intentionally by embracing God's good gift of life today and taking tangible steps toward the goals and hopes we've spent years only imagining. Participating in the present is the only way to engage more fully in the pursuit of our dreams.

UNCLUTTERING OUR LIVES

Do you ever wonder how in the world the stack of clutter builds up so quickly in our lives? Just when we think we've worked our way to the bottom of it, we look away for only a moment and it multiplies all over again.

Clutter piles up when we take on one more commitment, stay just a couple more hours at work, squeeze in one more appointment, or take part in one more activity. Our days are already full, but we somehow convince ourselves that much of the clutter is legitimate, so we take on a bit more. The overtime pay is certainly helpful; the new activity will most definitely open up friendships; the added commitment really is for a worthy cause or a good ministry.

As the clutter increases, our lives become more and more complicated, more complex, more of a juggling act than a gift. Somewhere in the midst of the accumulated stuff, we lose the moments. There is no time to see the world around us or breathe in the fresh breath of God's good and free gift of life when we're always running five minutes late. Before long, our very identity is caught up with the clutter, the busyness, the things that we do from morning to evening. Meanwhile, we remain oblivious to the moments of the journey.

From time to time, we simply need to pull back and re-evaluate the clutter that crowds our lives. In the same way we might do a heavy spring cleaning of our house, we need to examine why we do what we do in our daily lives and clean up or reorganize when necessary. Hauling away the clutter of our lives is essential if we are to experience the moments of this good gift of life.

It is incredibly freeing to get rid of things and obligations we only thought were necessary and to break the bondage of saying yes to every opportunity that is presented. Finding boundaries and discovering limits to what and how much we can do begins with simply recognizing that our identities are not found in how much we can accomplish and what we can produce. We are wholly grounded in being the graced and gifted children of a loving, life-giving God.

Getting rid of the clutter also challenges the tendency to live beyond our means. Societal pressures move many of us to purchase homes, cars, and other goods that subsequently require more money than we earn. So we take on extra jobs or clock more overtime hours. We can become so caught up in working more in order to have more that we end up missing life itself.

Remember Ecclesiastes? What if we end up achieving all the stuff but have no life? What if we pull in the money but we never spend time with friends and family? What if we drive a great car but only before the sun comes up and after the sun goes down? What if we have an impressive house, but only use it for sleeping? What if we buy a nice gift but never spend an hour or two just talking and laughing and dreaming with the person to whom we give it?

If our lives are so filled with stuff that we can never spend authentic time with people we love, then our lives have become too complex. Drinking a cup of coffee with a friend (for more than a minute or two), spending an hour just catching up, meeting an old friend at a restaurant, taking a Sunday afternoon drive, hiking along a trail, or playing a friendly round of tennis are not impositions in life. They comprise the moments of which life is made.

ENLIVENING THE SENSES

From time to time, I will make a quick trip up the street to get something at the neighborhood grocery store. I turn on the ignition, back up, pull out of my garage, go forward, drive up the street, park the car, go in, get what I need, stand in line, pay the cashier, go to my car, drive back down the street, open the garage door, pull into my garage, turn off the ignition, and go upstairs . . . without seeing, hearing, tasting, smelling, or really touching a thing!

I miss the bright red cardinal on the tree limb. I don't hear the sound of the children laughing and playing across the street. I don't feel the gentle breeze blowing through the trees as I walk into the store. I don't take in the aroma of the freshly baked bread. I am in such a hurry to get what

I need and return home that I fail to experience the moments of life.

From time to time, simply stopping long enough to ask, "What do I see? What do I hear? What do I smell? What do I taste? What do I feel?" will awaken our God-given senses that so easily become dull and will free us to embrace God's good gift of life.

CELEBRATING LIFE'S EVENTS

Events such as births, graduations, anniversaries, moves, promotions, marriages, retirements, and even funerals celebrate that God's good gift of life is not a stagnant and stale gift, but it is always moving forward in transition, change, and growth.

Discovering ways to join others in the celebration of these events allows us to participate in the rhythm and the music of life and *breathe in the moments.* We don't find ourselves living in the past when we celebrate these moments with people in our lives; we cradle fresh moments that we've never before experienced. Celebrations recognize that we live, change, grow, and face new moments all the time.

SHARING IN MEALS

One of the simplest times to listen to the music of life and discover the rhythm is while sharing meals with others. In our fast-paced society, food holds a very unique place. Particularly for the single adult, a cup of coffee and a breakfast bar on our drive to work, drive-thrus for lunch, and microwave dinners in front of the evening news can become characteristic.

For some in our society, food is a comfort in times of pain, while for others it is something to avoid in order to get fit. Still, for others it is the means to celebrate a great event. For many of us, eating a meal is a quick and brief diversion from the rest of the day—something we squeeze in before returning to the important things of life.

Eating meals together has been very significant through-out the history of God's people. The meal was seen as an ex-pression of God's good gift of life itself. For this reason, the custom of saying grace—praying a word of blessing and thanksgiving before eating—arose in the practice of God's people. The meal was not simply something done to survive or something to be avoided or something to be passed through quickly; it was indeed a moment—a gift from God.

Sometimes in our hurried manner of eating on the run or eating while standing at the kitchen sink or eating with our family gathered at the television with no interaction, we miss the gift that is discovered in the mealtime. The meal is more than a quick, five-minute experience to rush through so we can do more important things; it is a God-given *moment* during our day.

In those meals we share with other people, relationships are established. The bond is not based on how delectable the food tastes or on how much the meal cost; the meaning-ful interaction grows simply out of eating together. Meals can provide times of exuberant conversation or times of sheer silence. But eating with others is a recognition that we belong to a family. It is a way of saying, "You belong to me, and I belong to you."

The meal is more than simply a place to work through one more item of business, catch up on the latest gossip, share the latest news, or talk about life's great problems. While all of these may happen at our meals, the meal is ulti-mately a place of fellowship—a setting where we share life, blessings, gifts, and our common humanness at a table with another graced human being. *Experiencing* a meal allows us to inhale a gracious *moment* in God's good gift of life.

AN ETERNAL TOMORROW . . . BEGINNING TODAY

Sometimes the more discouraging moments of our life journeys resemble a ministry setting in which I participated not long ago. The leaders were giving everything they had to make sure that good, solid ministry was taking place. Indeed, they were providing outstanding models of the ministry of Christ; however, the fruit of their ministry just wasn't apparent.

The going really did get tough, and the difficulty of the situation brought a cloud of discouragement over many who were involved in the ministry. Some even considered giving up. One evening, as the ministry leaders gathered for prayer, one of our fellow ministry partners shared these words: "If we just hold on, there is something a whole lot better in the next life."

I really do understand and appreciate what our ministry leader was saying. He was pointing to the truth that life extends even beyond death. Certainly, the apostle Paul made it abundantly clear that even in death itself, Christians are not hopeless. Because of the resurrection of Jesus Christ, we, too, will be resurrected and live forever. Paul encouraged the people at Thessalonica by saying, "We do not want you to be uninformed, brothers and sisters, about those who have died, so that you may not grieve as others do who have no hope. For since we believe that Jesus died and rose again, even so, through Jesus, God will bring with him those who have died. . . . Therefore encourage one another with these words" (1 Thess. 4:13-14, 18).

To the Christians at Corinth, Paul announced, "Now if Christ is proclaimed as raised from the dead, how can some of you say there is no resurrection of the dead? If there is no resurrection of the dead, Christ has not been raised . . . If for this life only we have hoped in Christ, we are of all people most to be pitied" (1 Cor. 15:12-13, 19).

Throughout Scripture, there is hope beyond the present realities of brokenness, defeat, and discouragement. However, what my friend said reminded me of language that is prevalent among many Christians today—language that can easily cause us to miss experiencing the moments of God's good gift of life here and now. It is language that unintentionally, but most certainly, diminishes the significance and the beauty of the life that God presently gives us by saying that the present is simply a practice or even a rehearsal for *the real thing* that is to come in the future.

When the Bible speaks of life after we die, it never seeks to belittle or cheapen the goodness of the life God gives us now. The hope beyond our present lives is meant to encourage Christians to continue embracing God's good gift of life, holding on, enduring, and not giving up or giving in. Never was its motivation to see this life as some type of a practice session for the real life to come. This well-intentioned concept has become a misguided detour that causes Christians to miss the embrace of the good gift of life that God gives us today.

Our present life is not artificial; it is real! It is not a burden from God simply for us to endure as a test until we receive the real prize from God; life—here and now—is a gift from God to be received and experienced.

An honest hearing of Scripture reveals to us that the *real thing* of life is not an either/or situation. God's good gift of life is inclusive of both *now* and the *future*. How tragic it would be to wait for what God has in eternity and miss out on what God has for us right now—life that is real and beautiful and good—life in which God is very much an active player and participant.

While in no way detracting from the incredible significance of the truth that we will live beyond our present lives, we can affirm that life in the present is *more than* practice; it is more than a preparation for the real thing to come. Eternal life, abundant life, does not begin at death; it begins now and never ends. Life after death is the continuation of God's good gift of life that is already awake in us. We breathe it now; we will breathe it forever.

If living is *now* as well as tomorrow, how do we face and experience life in seasons of hurt? How can we make any sense out of natural disasters like hurricanes and famine, human pain found in poverty, disease, and hunger, and social brokenness such as alienation from friends, divorce, and the death of a loved one? How can we say that this life that God gives us is a *good* gift? Isn't our *only* hope in another life to come? Isn't this life honestly just holding on until we get something better?

Too often, religion itself can become a way of covering up the brokenness and the pain of human life. Our worship of God can function as a drug that gives us a high just long enough to get us through another week—just strong enough to make us forget the realities of human life for a few hours. Our hope in eternal life can even act as a way of repressing the grief of loss or masquerading the emotion that comes along with brokenness and suffering.

The God who gives us life provides something more authentic than a quick fix and more honest than a masquerade. The good of this gift of life is not that God takes away our humanness but that He puts on human flesh and participates in our humanness, weeping with us, suffering with us, even dying with us.

Seeing how God has so embraced human life—even human life that is suffering from the greatest wounds and grief possible, we must be all the more compelled to step into the lives of people around us who are disappointed, hungry, fearful, hurting, and broken. With a vision of the beautiful gift of this life, we are not wringing our hands saying, "The only hope for them is life after death." Rather, with this vision of life as gift, we become hope-givers and life-extenders to others in *this* good gift from God that we call life!

Along the journey, moments come—moments to breathe, inhale, embrace, and celebrate the good gift of life. In the midst of our busyness, caught up in yesterday's if onlys and tomorrow's what ifs, we have the moments of the here and the now to embrace. Even the darkest moments of the journey are not times to give up on the goodness of this gift of life; they indeed are moments to see God's embrace of life and know His participation in the moments with us.

6

Pausing for Sabbath Moments

Life had been in overdrive for the past two or three months and for at least three weeks, I was marking off the remaining days on my calendar until the upcoming spring break. The students thought *they* were looking forward to break; if they only knew how much I anticipated it!

As the week drew near, I caved to the pressure and started scheduling appointments and writing in new commitments on my calendar. I suddenly realized that I had filled almost every day of the break with a lot of busy-work. The old performance-driven air had filled my lungs once again and, sure enough, I found myself choking on it. However, one day in the week remained absolutely clear. I decided it would be my day to just stop and breathe.

The day finally arrived, and it was picture perfect. With a warm breeze blowing in the air, the skies were bright blue and the sun shone clearly. It was a day made for taking a walk around the neighborhood, playing in the dirt (my version of planting a few flowers), and getting a big glass of cold lemonade and sitting outside to read a book that wasn't on my have-to-read list.

Dressed in one of my comfortable, oversized, short-sleeved shirts, with a book in one hand and the glass of lemonade in the other, I kicked back on the lounge chair in my backyard. With the bright sun beaming down, I eventually put the book and glass down and drifted into a deep, restful sleep. I don't know how long I slept— probably a good half-hour—when suddenly a ringing telephone yanked me back into the world of the living.

Without even realizing what I was doing, I jumped up from the lounge chair and began clearing my throat as I ran inside to pick up the phone. I think I even said, "Hello . . . Hello," a couple of times on my way to the phone, just to make sure my voice didn't sound too groggy when I answered it.

I picked the receiver up and the person on the other end of the line asked the strangest question: "I didn't wake you, did I?" What was I supposed to say? I began thinking to myself in that split second, *I can't lie, but at the same time I sure don't want anyone to think that I'm home just sitting around being lazy! I mean it's the middle of the day. I should be up and alert and doing something productive. I could really be accomplishing a lot right now.*

Finally, after stuttering for a couple moments, I replied, "Oh, I was just taking a break; don't worry about it. What can I do for you?" Now I have to admit, I have wondered several times what the person on the other end of the line would have said if I had responded simply, "Yes." But I couldn't quite get a straight yes out of my lips; I needed to sound productive.

Why did I feel this way? Why is it that when we take a break in our busy lives we either feel guilty or we feel like we should be up doing more?

A COUNTERCULTURAL WORLD

The other day, I passed another vehicle on the highway. I looked over and saw the driver consumed in everything *but* driving. A telephone wire hung from his ear as he chatted with great animation. At the same time, he was checking e-mail and text messages on another gadget that was attached to his front windshield. In between bites of his burger and fries that were conveniently stashed on the dashboard, he would reach up and type a message—all while trying to keep his eyes on the road ahead.

We are certainly not the first society or the first generation to be performance-driven. However, as technology booms, we are becoming more and more like machines. It is almost as if we are playing a game to see who can accomplish the most tasks at any given moment.

Into the midst of our work-oriented world comes a rather odd biblical teaching in one of the Ten Commandments that many of us memorized as children. We probably memorized something like this: *Remember the Sabbath day and keep it holy.* It's sort of easy for religious people to shrug their shoulders and say, "Well, I go to church every Sunday," and then move on to the next commandment. In fact, many of us feel that we actually embody this commandment because we teach Sunday School, conduct children's church, sing in the choir, prepare for church dinners, and attend afternoon meetings *in addition* to going to church.

Whatever the reason, singles can particularly find our schedules on Sundays loaded from the time we get up early to finish preparing a lesson, to the time we finally go to bed late at night after spending a couple of hours with other singles at the local restaurant. The busyness in which we find ourselves is certainly found in good things—ministry, discipleship, leadership, fellowship. Nevertheless, it is ironic that the day of rest leaves many of us more exhausted and burned out on Monday than on any other day of the week.

Among all of the moments that are a part of the journey of life, the Sabbath moment is an essential part of this gift of life. Although these moments are vital, they seem to be very difficult to actually experience. So how do we ever really experience Sabbath moments as God intended them to be experienced in our lives?

The answer is found in rediscovering just what the Sabbath command is about. The instruction is actually expressed in three simple words that give us a sense of just what Sabbath is about: *remember, sanctify,* and *stop.*

The first admonition is not "Sanctify the Sabbath" but "*Remember* to sanctify the Sabbath." Why *remember?* In a performance-driven world that works 24/7, it is very easy to become absent-minded and simply forget that life is not ultimately about how much we can accomplish in a seven-day week. The directive on this command in Deut. 5:12 actually replaces the word "remember" with a similar word that gives an even deeper understanding of what it means for us to intentionally remember to set aside moments of Sabbath. The word literally means "guard" or "watch over carefully." Unless we intentionally and purposefully put the purpose of Sabbath at the forefront of our memories, we will become preoccupied with the clutter and busyness of life and let it go by without ever experiencing it.

Remembering leads us to sanctify the Sabbath. Sanctifying something means setting it apart; it is taking something of ordinary and mundane use and making it extraordinary. *Remembering to sanctify* a particular moment of our lives means making absolutely certain that the moment is set apart from everything else; it's supposed to be different from all of the other busy moments of our lives.

When we hear we should *remember to sanctify* the Sabbath, much probably comes to mind. Most of us already have many preconceived ideas about the *Sabbath.* The concept is loaded with notions that range all the way from taking a nap, to going to worship, to avoiding this practice or that place. Sadly, most of our popular ideas have very little to do with what Sabbath literally means.

Perhaps the best way to understand the root meaning of this word is to place it in the context in which it is often used today. You can see this word repeated over and over again on a red, octagonal-shaped sign at the corner of intersecting roads. The word simply means "to stop, to quit"—to cease from what we are presently doing. Experiencing a Sabbath moment is simply ceasing from the ordinary, everyday, routine activities of productivity and accomplishment. The word has nothing to do with performance-oriented activity. Rather than *doing*, Sabbath is primarily about *not doing*.

SABBATH . . . WHY NOT?

The whole idea sounds so great! Why *wouldn't* we take a Sabbath? The instructions provided in Exodus, Deuteronomy, and in Jesus' teachings not only give important rationale as to why we should have Sabbath moments in our lives but also reflect underlying excuses we make, delusions we have, and struggles we face in authentically experiencing a Sabbath lifestyle.

Struggle 1: "I Just Don't Have Time." In partnering with God to take a Sabbath, we discover a struggle common to many of us. For various reasons, some legitimate and others illegitimate, we convince ourselves that we just don't have the time to stop and experience Sabbath moments.

In the Sabbath instruction found in Exodus, the need for a Sabbath is based upon *God's identity.* After six days of creative work, it says that God looked at all He had done, announced that it was very good, and He *stopped!* (20:11). He did not continue the same routine of the previous six days, but rather, He stopped to enjoy and celebrate all that had taken place. The Creator—the One upon whom everything within the universe is utterly dependent—stops! And the creation that He has created continues to exist; it continues to survive; life goes on!

Now just think about this for a minute. If the Creator of the universe can actually stop and all is fine, then why do I think that the world is dependent upon me continuing to work 24/7 with no stops in between? If even God can stop, then surely I can stop . . . unless I no longer see life as a gift from God but as a product of my own labors. As I honestly and authentically recognize and celebrate that I am not the ultimate source of my life but that this life is a sheer gift from the God of love, I can join Him and . . . *stop!*

Because life is a gift and God is the ultimate Giver of this good gift, the need to stop and find moments to celebrate life as a sheer gift is engrained into the very fabric of who we are as God's creatures. The Sabbath is not a time-filler that God set up for our lives when we have nothing else to do. The need for Sabbath is interwoven into the very fabric of what it means for us to be creatures and not creators, human and not divine.

Struggle 2: Forgetting Our God-Given Identity. In the Sabbath instructions in Deut. 5:15, the need for Sabbath is based upon *our identity* as people who base our self-understanding upon what God has accomplished in our lives.

Remembering that at one time they had been slaves in Egypt, our ancestors realized that God had completely changed their identity when He brought them across the Red Sea. No longer were they slaves whose identities were based upon their production of pyramids and temples. They were now grounded in the radical alternative of freedom. No longer were they defined by work; they were now defined by grace.

Coming face-to-face with the radical alternative of a God who freely parts the waters and frees us from an identity based upon how much of the pyramid we completed today unveils a new identity based upon grace. What better way to acknowledge our God-given identity than to *stop* and receive that gift freely.

When we forget that we are the blessed children of God and that all of life is a sheer gift, we live under the delusion that we are what we produce; we are what we can accomplish. Oddly, we even tend to relish a perverted form of self-importance or value by remaining on call and working 24/7. The more pride we take in our busyness, the less we tend to set apart stop times—Sabbath moments.

Struggle 3: Learning to Truly Stop. One Sabbath day, Jesus and His disciples were walking through a field and became hungry. So, the disciples began plucking some grain (Mark 2:23). The religious leaders who were strict observers of the

Sabbath began questioning why Jesus' disciples were *working* on the Sabbath. Probably out of good but misdirected hearts, these religious men had turned God's gracious gift of Sabbath into an act of human performance. While the Sabbath was designed to celebrate the gift-nature of life itself, they came to see it as a series of dos and don'ts—in other words, as one more series of achievements.

Responding to this crowd's judgment on His disciples, Jesus made an amazing announcement: "The Sabbath was made for man, not man for the Sabbath" (v. 27, NIV). God never intended the Sabbath to be one more straightjacket into which human beings must squeeze and perform.

In the good intentions of this religious crowd, we see a struggle that is common to us all. We are so trained to produce and accomplish that even when we do stop and breathe in Sabbath moments, our first question is often, "What should I do or not do?" We are so accustomed to the performance mentality that the Sabbath can simply become just like everything else in life—one more thing to do, one more task to complete, one more accomplishment to carry out.

However, as God's gift to us, the Sabbath is a regular, repeated exercise in which we simply receive and embrace life as God's pure and simple gift to us. It is that experience in life in which we pause long enough to acknowledge that the life we live is not the result of our own work or productivity but is the result of the grace and goodness of a life-breathing God. Sabbath moments are physical demonstrations that we comprehend that God is the Life-Giver and we are only the life-receivers. The inability to stop, to receive, and to experience Sabbath is a very vivid sign that we are taking ourselves far too seriously, even when our work and labors are for the very best intentions in the world.

BECOMING PEOPLE OF SABBATH MOMENTS

At the outset, it really does become important for those of us who are active, churchgoing people to understand the relationship (and sometimes the lack of relationship) between Sabbath moments and going to church. Busyness in the life of the church can all too easily substitute for *experiencing* the Sabbath. Certainly, we have our times of gathering for corporate worship, and God's Word clearly admonishes us to gather with believers to worship the Lord and celebrate the astonishing new life of resurrection on resurrection day. However, the observation of Sabbath is not simply another day for religious people to perform.

Sabbath moments are more than a change of religious scenery. Corporate worship, particularly what we experience every Sunday, provides a regathering and replenishing experience in our lives. It invigorates; it enlivens; it renews; and it reminds us who we are in light of who God is.

However, for many of us who are actively involved in the life and service of the church, Sabbath moments outside of our regular corporate worship times are of immeasurable significance. A full slate of activities on Sunday is not a substitute for God's desire for us to stop and receive life as His good gift.

Sabbath is first a mind-set. Sabbath minds stand in wonder and awe of life as a pure gift. Sabbath minds humbly acknowledge that we are not the source of life, and they relax in the assurance that God is the trustworthy and dependable Giver of life.

Sabbath eyes see the beauty of life that is often overlooked and missed in our busy, performance-oriented lifestyles. They see personal accomplishments and achievements not as life itself but as fruit that flows out of the already-present gift of life.

Admittedly, this type of mind-set and vision is completely countercultural. It flies in the face of seeing life primarily as an opportunity to produce a little more and achieve a little higher.

Sabbath moments must become deliberate; they will not just happen. Sabbath moments must become deliberate and premeditated in our lives. We must think about them in advance, even plan for them. Good intentions do not create Sabbath moments. They should not become optional or second-place in our lives even if a better offer comes along. For some of us who are driven by written schedules and calendars, we might even need to write them down . . . and then stick to them.

Sabbath moments are creative experiences and expressions of the reality that life is a gift. Taking Sabbath moments requires some form of stopping the normal routines of our lives. If we are students, then our common routines as students will stop. If we are professionals, then our customary practices will be altered. If we are care-givers to a child or to a parent, then our everyday schedule will be interrupted in some way. In order to be set apart from the commonplace ventures of life, if possible, they might incorporate a change of scenery.

Sabbath moments may be very brief, or they may be rather extended. A Sabbath moment can experience and express the beauty of God's good gift of life in a few minutes just as well as it can for several hours or even days. However, they should be regular. In other words, one extended Sabbath moment per year (such as a week-long vacation) does not satisfy for the full year.

We might find a Sabbath moment in the midst of listening to and even singing along with, music. Or perhaps we place ourselves in a favorite spot in God's creation and just allow our eyes and ears to soak in the beauty and the goodness. Or maybe we laugh and share in conversation with someone with whom we are totally free to be ourselves. A Sabbath moment can happen while sitting alone in our favorite chair reflecting on the gift of life. They will often find themselves in places that we have discovered to be a refuge —a sheltering place that provides us with a sense of security.

As diverse as Sabbath moments may be, they should be times when we simply celebrate the goodness of God.

Sabbath moments serve as signposts for our lives. The Sabbath serves as a repeated reminder that we are not simply slaves to tasks and assignments. Sabbath moments allow us to see with clearer minds what needs to be done in the coming days realistically and honestly.

Some of us learn the art of saying no quite early. Others,

whether we are living under the superhero syndrome or a cloud of guilt for not doing more, seem to never quite acquire the ability to say no. Sabbath moments keep us from overloading our lives with busyness for the sake of busyness.

Sabbath moments are not perpetual—but the Sabbath mindset is. In my early years as a professor, I had an unforgettable encounter with a young freshman student just after spring break. She had worked extremely hard throughout the first several months of college. Like many first-year students, she had overloaded her life with busyness. Not only was she taking a full load of classes, but she was also involved in several campus ministries, a choir, a couple of intramural athletic competitions, and working 20 hours a week on top of all that.

The Monday following spring break, she came running into my office, shut the door, drew a big breath, and exclaimed, "Chaplain Green! I have finally discovered God's will for my life!" Naturally, I was thrilled to hear that she was working through issues of God's guidance in her journey, so I asked her, "What is it?" She responded, "I have never been more fulfilled than I was this past week of spring break. You see, I just went home and did nothing. I slept in until noon and spent the rest of the day relaxing. It was so fulfilling!" Then as a beaming smile spread across her face, she continued, "God's will for me is a lifetime of spring breaks."

I have to admit, I was speechless. After a few seconds of awkward silence, I responded in what I hoped was a constructive way. But now, even years later, I can still see that beaming smile and that sense of certainty as she announced God's will for her life: perpetual spring break.

One problem with seeing all of life as a Sabbath is that it just isn't, and if we convince ourselves that it is, we will never have the purposeful break in our lives that Sabbath is intended to give.

Sabbath is a gift to be extended to others. Throughout the biblical instructions for Sabbath, this gift of God is not only to be experienced by ourselves but also is to be extended to others. Extending Sabbath to others goes so much further than simply giving a little time off to our employees. It is giving time off to family, friends, associates, even our coworkers at church. It is refusing to burden others down by using superhero tactics ("Oh, you can certainly do this"). Or by using guilt tactics ("If you don't do this, no one else will"). It is recognizing that in the same way that we are not defined by performance and accomplishment, we cannot define others by what they perform and accomplish.

Part Three
THE RELEASE—
EXTENDING LIFE AS A GIFT

From her gentle embrace,
She now began ever so methodically
To open up both hands . . . one finger at a time.

No longer with a tight fist but with hands wide open,
She meticulously began stretching out her folded arms.

Although they were once folded tightly across her chest,
She proceeded to slowly move her arms straight out to
*   her side*
In a posture of openness and trust.

As if she were releasing the prize she had discovered
To anyone who would take it from her,
She was prepared to embrace everyone in sight
Just as much as she had embraced her invisible gift.

She thought nobody saw her dancing the childlike
*   dance—*
She thought nobody else could hear the music that she
*   heard.*
I saw her dance . . . I heard the music . . .
And my life was changed as my heart began dancing to
*   the music as well!*

7

Community: Making Accommodations

The desire to keep the gift of life and make it our own personal possession reminds me of trying to catch shining lightning bugs as a child. The mysterious off-and-on glow and the warmth and frivolity of springtime evenings made for thrilling moments of leaping into the air and capturing the electrified insects. It was exhilarating to bring my closed hands back down, slowly open my fingers, and peek at the twinkling light.

As a five-year-old, I went outdoors one evening and decided to capture as many lightning bugs as I could. I thought it would be magical to create my own living light bulb by placing the insects inside a jar. It seemed like a brilliant idea to me.

That evening, I took the jar full of life inside and placed it beside my bed. Sure enough, as I went to sleep, the lights continued to blink on and off. However, by the time morning came, my light bulb had become complete darkness. All of the electricity that shone inside the jar the night before was gone. What was once filled with life and light was now motionless and dark.

When life is captured, preserved, and contained, it becomes snuffed out and lifeless. As much as we might desire to hold and preserve the beautiful gift of life for ourselves, it can only remain a gift as it is freed from our own grasp and released to others. Only when life is relinquished and shared does it remain the gracious, invigorating gift of life. A contained life becomes like a stuffy, moldy room; it chokes all who enter the small, damp space of self-preservation and can create a feeling of doom. But as we embrace life and release it freely to others, we discover an airiness and spaciousness in our own lives that opens us up to receive even more.

Nevertheless, we have an engrained tendency to cling so tightly to life that we nearly squeeze the, well . . . *life* out of it. Sometimes it comes in the fear we have to step into unfamiliar territory and relationships. Life would just be a lot easier, it seems, if we could stay put in our own little isolated and private worlds with our familiar surroundings and relationships. We've worked hard to get this world constructed just like we like it; why would we want to step outside of it? We convince ourselves that we are self-sufficient here. We've learned to depend upon ourselves, and isn't that enough?

At other times, we just find it really difficult to become vulnerable enough to share life with other people in an open and honest way. It feels safer to stay inside our own guarded world where we can't get hurt. It's a lot simpler to keep everybody else at a safe distance and maintain our guard . . . just in case. *What if they don't like me? What if I don't fit in? What if they don't accept me? What if I'm rejected? What if . . . What if . . . What if . . .* So we hold on to what we've got, put it in a jar, screw the lid on tightly, and preserve it.

Embracing life and never opening our arms to extend it to those all around us is deadly. Placing life inside a protective container with a preserving lid on top only results in a rude awakening the next morning: light becomes darkness and the sweet aroma of life becomes the stench of death.

Perhaps this reality is exactly what Jesus meant when He said that those who hold on to their lives—those who live to preserve themselves and what they have and who they know —will lose it.

At its heart, relinquishing our lives to others requires

that we experience the vulnerability of life lived in authentic relationship with other human beings. Here we discover the love found in mutually shared community with other warm-blooded people who dream and laugh and cry and fail and hope, just like we do. We discover the peace of letting go of what we claim others owe us and no longer allow those debts to cast the long shadows of payback, cynicism, and anger over our lives.

The dance of life does not stop with taking our arms up to the air and then holding them tightly to our chest; the childlike dance is not complete until one more fluid motion takes place. With our hands clutched tightly to our chest, we must proceed to open up our arms widely as we extend our lives to all who are around us. And ironically, with arms outstretched and hands wide open, we are ready once again to reach to the sky . . . one more time ready to receive the good gift of a childlike life!

TURNING OFF THE "NO VACANCY" SIGN

Driving up the little two-lane highway, every single neon sign screamed, *NO Vacancy . . . NO Vacancy . . . NO Vacancy*. I proceeded for several miles, but the bright signs of rejection kept lighting up the night. In fact, they seemed to get brighter and brighter the further I drove. What was going on? I guessed maybe it was a convention or something. All I knew was that every place was filled; there was no room for me in that town!

I was nearly on the other end of town when I saw one more sign that read just like all the others: NO Vacancy. As I passed by, suddenly, the bright pink neon NO flashed off. I saw the one word I had been looking for all evening: Vacancy. In the silent emptiness of my car, I announced out loud to no one but myself, "Vacancy! Vacancy! They have room for me!"

Sometimes the journey of life seems to be an awful lot like driving through a strange, out-of-the-way town with no room. How often in our performance-driven culture, where the focus is on our individual accomplishments and achievements, do we see the NO Vacancy signs hanging brightly outside of people's lives? Sometimes, it even hangs on our own lives. Our popular songs seem to say it; our heroic stories depict it; our lifestyles portray it. In a society that is mesmerized by finding the weakest link, removing the least favorable bachelor or bachelorette from the scene, and forming flimsy alliances that last only until our strategy requires kicking that allied friend from the household, we have just come to accept the NO Vacancy sign in this world.

However, human beings are created for life in community rather than life in isolation. The type of community for which we are created is not simply one that finds a friend or two and then locks the door; rather, we are created for a community that keeps the door wide open to others . . . it keeps the "Vacancy" sign lit.

Throughout the story of God's creation of the world, God repeatedly evaluates His work with the declaration that it is good—meaning, it is appropriate, it is fitting. In other words, the light is appropriate to overcome darkness; the land is appropriate to overcome the seas; the sun and moon, the birds and fish, and the land animals are all appropriate to fill up what God has made.

But as we mentioned in chapter 1, a point comes for the first time in the story of God's creative work when He announces that something is *not* good; there is something that is just not appropriate within His creation. He declares, *It is not appropriate that human beings should be alone.* God proceeds to announce that the human being needs a "helper." This word "helper" does not convey the idea of a subordinate or second in command. In fact, it is the same word that is used in the Bible for God himself as He stands in relationship to His people ready to assist them in times of need. This *helper* is further described by God as corresponding to the human being, much like a reflection in a mirror.

The story of the creation of male and female follows. By

its end, the story leads to the first song of the Bible—a wedding song. Obviously, this story very vividly demonstrates the biblical understanding of marriage and sexuality in which the coming together of one male and one female is an experience of intimacy where two separate human beings become one flesh. What a mysterious, sacred, and beautiful understanding of the husband-wife relationship.

However, this story also portrays something broader than the perspective of marriage. It is a portrait of what it means for us to be human. Human beings cannot live in isolation from other human beings. While marriage is one expression of this intimacy, shared life with other humans is not limited to marriage.

Unfortunately, the popular media, society at large, and even the church can feed the mindset that says authentic and genuine intimacy can only be experienced in the marriage relationship. Good friends and well-meaning family members who simply want the best for their single friend or family member can unintentionally represent the unmarried life as a partial life that needs quickly to be made complete. As a result, single adults can easily buy into this misleading and false concept and make rushed decisions to marry by a certain age or quickly remarry following a divorce or the death of a spouse. The good of being human is not grounded in saying "I do"; the good of being human is sharing life, community, fellowship, and intimacy with other human beings.

Within this broader context of shared life, the God-ordained relationship of marriage may take place. However, the intimacy of our humanness is not exclusive to marriage. Certainly, Jesus, Paul, and a multitude of others in the Bible, and throughout the history of Christianity, were not married, yet they experienced the fullness of human life as they shared life in community with other people.

God's announcement at the beginning of creation that it is just not appropriate that human beings live this good gift of life alone is ultimately God's declaration that the Vacancy sign should be turned on in all the relationships of our lives. God is always a hospitable God, a God who always has one more chair at the table for one more person. In the same way, He calls us to be people who are ready to add one more chair to the table, accommodate one more person, and say, "Come on in . . . I'm open!"

That night, I pulled up to the hotel with the bright VACANCY sign, went inside, and asked, "Do you have a room for me?" The response is imbedded in my mind, "Yes, there's room for you here; we can definitely accommodate you."

MAKING ACCOMMODATIONS FOR OTHERS: RENOVATION TIME

The contrast between Vacancy and NO Vacancy is seen in many neighborhoods on the one night each year when kids of all ages come out of their houses dressed up in costumes and look for goodies by knocking on doors and exclaiming, "Trick or treat!" Have you ever driven through a neighborhood on that night? It's so obvious which households are saying, "Come on up; we've got something for you." Not only is the porch light on, but often, the floodlights are on, candles are burning, and people are standing on the front porch. It's also clear which houses are saying, "Don't even think of knocking on my door!" The lights are out, curtains are drawn, and the doors are tightly shut.

In our individual-oriented, performance-driven, competitive world, we need to look once again at the blueprints of our lives and explore ways that renovation might take place so that our ability to welcome and accommodate those around us is expanded.

TEAR DOWN THE WALLS!

As we reach our early adult years, a cultural rite-of-passage demands we get out there on our own. Individualism becomes a way of life that is expected of us, and any sense of needing others outside of ourselves is viewed as childish, immature, even *unhealthy*.

When life situations, such as divorce, death, or the loss of loved ones and friends, throw us back into being alone, the sheer panic of having to do things on our own can create a strong and determined sense of, *Since no one else will look out for me, then I've got to look out for myself.*

If people in our lives in whom we have particularly placed our trust, such as family, friends, work associates, or even fellow church members, take advantage of our vulnerability, we can develop a defensive and even cynical position in all future relationships. In order to not be hurt again, we squash the vulnerability that is necessary to allow people into our lives. We can develop a calloused and even cold approach to sharing life with other people. It just seems much simpler to live life on our own, only turning to other people when absolutely necessary. We hang the Sorry . . . I'm Closed sign on our lives and live with no vacancy for anyone else.

The disintegration of walls that often took a lifetime to build begins with recognizing that we are created to be in relationship with other people. From God's perspective, it is not good or appropriate that we live in isolation behind high and thick walls. Mature independence is not living outside of relationships but living responsibly and mutually *with* other people.

One of the problems is that vulnerability is too often confused with gullibility. Gullible people naively approach life without using the minds that God gave them. They enter into relationships and situations without thinking or praying over implications and ramifications or consulting others who can give wisdom. Vulnerability involves the risk of opening our lives, our minds, and our hearts to other people.

Just as opening our arms to embrace someone lowers the defensive position of self-protection, opening our lives to others removes the defensive walls that keep others out. In becoming vulnerable, we refuse to run from human relationships simply out of the fear of being hurt. We extend

patience and trust in others that believe, hope, and endure.
We come out of the back room where we have been hiding,
and we turn the lights back on. We dare to say, "Come on in
. . . I'm open."

ENLARGE THE ROOM!

As our world becomes increasingly global and we are ex-
posed to greater diversity, we may find ourselves making our
homes in comfortable little corners of the world with people who look and think and act and believe just as we do.
The familiarity somehow feels safer. Those on the outside
are easily labeled by their politics or their race or their gender or their cultural backgrounds or even their religious affiliation.

Life in this world has not changed much. Two thousand
years ago, classifications based on everything from gender,
to socioeconomic status to religion were made and people
were identified by their groups and associations. No wonder
Jesus made such a stir when He dared to open His life to
others by stepping over the line to eat a meal with the self-
serving tax collector, reach out with a warm hand to the
sore-ridden leper, and share in intimate conversation with
the Samaritan woman with a string of ex-husbands. None of
these people belonged to His group, yet there was enough
room in His life to allow them to come near.

It only makes sense that Jesus told a story about a father
who had two sons in Luke 15. The one son, the rebel who
ran away from home and spent all of his inheritance on a
frivolous life, returned to his father saying, "I'm not worthy,
so I'll stay out in the field with the hired hands and work for
my food." But this father had a house—a life—large enough
to receive the wayward son back. He kept the house open for
him; there was room inside. There was vacancy in his life!

The other son was the good son, the faithful son, the son
who had always done just what his father desired. Upon
hearing that his father had made room for the young, rebel-

lious son, he seemed to mimic the old western saying, "This town (this house) isn't big enough for both of us."

But the father saw it very differently. His house was certainly big enough for the loyal son as well as the rebellious son. The father basically said, "There's more than enough room inside for you. Come on in; everything I have is yours!" The sign was clear on this father's house: Vacancy! Come in . . . I'm Open! The question was not whether the father had room; the question was whether the brothers were willing to live in the spacious house that had more than enough room for both of them.

The church at Corinth is another great biblical example of the struggle to make room for others—particularly those who do not think, look, or act just like everyone else. The church members lived by the premise that individual acts of spiritual strength and wisdom were the foundation for a walk with God. As a result, the church was quickly divided into factions based on strengths and weaknesses. Some aligned themselves with one leader while others were more attracted to another. The NO Vacancy quickly went up and the lights of hospitality went dark. Church dinners even turned into contests to see who could be first in line!

In 1 Corinthians, the apostle Paul addresses the same struggles that keep the lights off and the NO Vacancy signs on in our lives today. We have an amazing tendency to believe we are inferior or weaker or just can't live up to what other people are capable of doing or being. We see how all the other pieces of the puzzle interlock and then decide that the puzzle piece of our own life just doesn't fit. So we conclude that we are not needed.

Using the image of the human body, Paul describes the absolute danger of a skewed viewpoint on this issue. "If the foot would say, 'Because I am not a hand, I do not belong to the body,' that would not make it any less a part of the body. And if the ear would say, 'Because I am not an eye, I do not belong to the body,' that would not make it any less a part of the body. If the whole body were an eye, where would the hearing be?" (1 Cor. 12:15-17).

In some situations, we make accusations of weakness not about ourselves but about someone else. But Paul again makes a very intriguing point when he observes that "the members of the body that seem to be weaker are indispensable, and those members of the body that we think less honorable we clothe with greater honor" (vv. 22-23).

A second problem with which Paul deals is the opposite of inferiority. A sense of *superiority* can move us to withdraw and live life apart from others in a way that says, *I can do it on my own. I don't need anyone else. I have all I need to make it!* This approach even infiltrates much of popular Christian thinking today. Consider the songs we sing, such as, "Though no one join me, still I will follow." The heroic survival mode is often praised as the sign of ultimate trust in God.

However, Paul says to the community at Corinth, "The eye cannot say to the hand, 'I have no need of you,' nor again the head to the feet, 'I have no need of you'" (v. 21). We cannot fully understand our individual *selves* apart from something much larger. I don't just *need* others; I *must* have others. Shared life with others is not just God's bonus; shared life with others is God's design from the beginning.

Finally, Paul addresses the need to enlarge our living space. This mind-set is the frequent tendency to clone others so that they are just like us. He writes, "If the whole body were an eye, where would the hearing be? If the whole body were hearing, where would the sense of smell be? . . . If all were a single member, where would the body be?" (vv. 17, 19).

Most people want some type of life together with others; however, we do it artificially. We attempt to discover and experience artificial community through politics or religion or special interests. We do this by finding the lowest common denominator that brings us together and simply focusing on it.

Enlarging the space of our lives accepts the beautiful reality that the body is comprised of diverse members—eyes, ears, nose, mouth, fingers, feet, and on and on. Rather than ignoring the diverse nature of those with whom we share life and attempting to find the common elements, life in Christian community recognizes and celebrates each individual part and represents the manner in which each part is interconnected to the whole.

Ears and eyes and nose and mouth converse, listen, interact, appreciate, and share life together! We belong to something bigger than just ourselves with our own tastes and interests and pasts and dreams, and in the midst of this larger whole we live a mutually shared life with those who are like us . . . and those who are not.

Bring in a Huge Table! After the walls come down and rooms are expanded, the renovation of our life space continues by bringing in a huge table. A huge table? Sure, a table at which we can eat and laugh and cry and dream and hope and pray and trust and imagine and agree and agree to disagree and . . . share life! Bringing a huge table into our lives is a purposeful, deliberate, intentional step of sharing life with other people.

When I lived in Ohio, several hundred single adults gathered from all over the greater Cincinnati area every Friday night. At 7:00, we shared in worship and Bible study for a good hour and a half. Afterward, we gathered in the gym for light refreshments and fellowship. That lasted about another hour and a half.

Once the clock hit 10 P.M., anywhere from 50 to 100 of us would head to the local pancake house. The workers always knew we were coming . . . right on time! As soon as we arrived, we took all of the tables meant for four people and zigzagged them through the restaurant, creating one giant table.

I think we did a pretty good job of tipping each week, but we actually didn't order food. At the most, we got something to drink and then sat around the table and talked, sometimes for hours. We laughed over the funny moments of someone's day, cried over the defeats of another person's week, dreamed of the possibilities for someone's job, and prayed for the hurts of somebody else's family. Oh, from time to time, we'd even argue over the latest political debate.

In the course of the night, some offered to help fix plumbing and others volunteered to bake some bread. Some encouraged the discouraged and others gave advice on what to do next. From time to time, I would look around at the crazy maze of tables. Nineteen-year-olds sat with 40-year-olds who sat with 75-year-olds. Age just didn't matter there.

Single dads and single moms, widows and widowers, never-married professionals, university students, and high school dropouts were mixed with everyone else. Diverse denominations with diverse manners of expressing worship to God were scattered around the table that had more than enough room for everybody . . . regardless of their denominational affiliation. Some of the extroverts hopped from one seat to another, always initiating new conversation. Those on the introverted side just sat at the table and listened . . . but they listened with the gleam of the gift of life in their eyes and the joy of shared life in their hearts.

The huge table was about more than eating and drinking together; it was about intentionally sharing life together. It was about purposefully putting ourselves in a situation where there were other people—real live human beings who could also laugh and cry and dream and hope! It was about learning to recognize that these other people were a part of me and I was a part of them. It was about discovering that I was indeed an individual but that my individuality could only be celebrated in the context of something bigger than just me. It was about putting action to the nice idea that someday I would share life with other people—it was about actually sharing life with other people!

Around that huge table, we experienced what Paul described to the church at Corinth: "If one member suffers, all suffer together with it; if one member is honored, all rejoice together with it" (1 Cor. 12:26). There at the huge table of shared life, we continued the dance of life by extending our arms and our hearts away from our chests and toward to each other!

Install Large Picture Windows on Every Wall! Genuine community is never exclusive. It always looks outside of itself. So before the renovation of our life-space is complete, it might be a good idea to cut big holes in the outer walls and install large, clear picture windows so we can look out and others can see in.

The longer we share in community with close friends, Bible study groups, work associates, neighbors, and even fellow church members, we develop common languages, stories, songs, and even inside jokes. These shared memories provide incredible comfort and intimacy to those of us who belong. But they can also *un*intentionally serve as a way of keeping others outside the circle of our friendships and intimate relationships.

It becomes particularly easy for people of faith to find a safe place and inadvertently close the shutters on the windows so that nobody else can look in and we don't have to look out. It's just comfortable to have our common friends. Singles ministries can very easily fall prey to this trap. We find people in our ministry with whom we can feel safe and even vulnerable. Letting someone new in could threaten that safe place. Who knows? That person might disappoint or hurt us.

In the same way that the space of our individual lives needs to remain open to the renovations of tearing down walls and enlarging rooms, the various groups in which we find ourselves—such as our families, work associates, church groups, neighborhood associations—should make every effort to keep the windows wide open for others to see and feel welcomed. Groups that turn in upon themselves tend to become suffocating and lifeless. In seeking to preserve their lives, they indeed lose the very life they once had. Groups that intentionally explore ways to expand the space in their shared lives continue a fresh liveliness and joy that self-serving and exclusive relationships quickly lose.

MAKING PLANS FOR THE RENOVATION

In the same way that a home renovation never just happens, rarely does shared life just happen. Community building is intentional. As we come to recognize the necessity of sharing life with other people and hearing the good Giver of life say, *It's just not appropriate for humans to be alone*, we dare to risk the vulnerability of sharing life with others. With God's grace, we proceed to tear down the walls and enlarge the space. We dare to make room for those people who might look at life differently, talk differently, appear differently, and speak differently. We move beyond the inferiority that says, "I don't belong," or the superiority that exclaims, "I can do it alone." We come to celebrate our individuality in light of something larger than ourselves. We dare to bring in a huge table—intentionally and purposefully finding spaces and places in our lives for others. And then we proceed to put picture windows throughout our lives so that we can always keep our eyes outside—refusing to settle for the stale, suffocating life of exclusive shared community.

8

Letting Go of Debts

It was a great workout for a full half hour. Everything was going smoothly until the treadmill on which I was slowly jogging became a possessed machine. Suddenly, as if it had a mind of its own, the speed increased rapidly from a nice, easy jog of 5 miles per hour to 7. Then to 9. Then on to 11.

I had no idea what was happening. As far as I knew, this was some type of gimmick the local fitness center was using to challenge people like me who were in a fitness rut.

The treadmill suddenly slowed down even more quickly than it sped up. In a matter of seconds, it went from a rapid 11 miles per hour to a turtle-pace of just 3 and then, to make matters worse, the incline rose sharply and fell again.

At this point, I reached out and held on to grips wondering what in the world was coming next. The more the treadmill moved to its own pace, the more determined I was to hold on! Several minutes later, it started all over again. This time, even more rapidly, the pace shot up from 5 to 11, 13, 15, 17 miles per hour! With my arms now flapping wildly in the wind, I was running a mad dash! Most people would've jumped off by now, and yet, I was stubbornly determined not to let this rebellious piece of equipment dictate my afternoon workout.

Finally, the self-determined contraption threw its last punch. This time there was no warning; there was no gentle slowdown. In a split second, the treadmill went from 17 to zero! I had only one way to go—over the top, straight in front, and flat on my belly.

When I got back to the office later that afternoon, sore and bruised, I gingerly sat down at my desk and picked up the telephone to answer a call. Within moments, it felt like I was back on the treadmill. It was even worse this time because it was no longer a machine pushing my buttons and manipulating my emotions, it was a real person—someone I called a friend.

From the voice on the other end of the telephone came words and emotions and sentiments that I could not believe. Clearly, he had misunderstood me, but it did not make any difference to him. Obviously, he had gotten the wrong idea, but that just didn't seem important. Certainly, what he was saying was not correct, but he thought it was, and that was all that mattered.

When I hung up the phone, I did not know what to think or do. Really, I didn't even know how to feel. Almost every emotion ran through my mind: anger, frustration, hurt, dismay, shock, disappointment, sadness. His words continued to play over and over in my mind. The feelings that he expressed burned hotly to the very core of me. How could he assume that? How could he say that?

I grabbed my keys off the desk, walked out to my car, rolled down the windows, turned on the radio, got on the highway, and drove . . . and drove . . . and drove. I was going nowhere.

If only life's manipulators were as harmless as runaway treadmills and even brash phone conversations, life would be pretty simple. However, life is ultimately lived in community with people whom we have come to trust, love, and count on. Consequently, we run the risk of becoming frus-

trated, disillusioned, hurt, and angered by words and actions of people to the point that they can dictate and control anything from a brief moment in our day to the remainder of our lives.

Certainly, our emotions and thoughts can be impacted
by events as small as a slow driver pulling in front of us on
the highway, a person in front of us at the grocery store having a week's worth of groceries in the seven items or less
line, or spam e-mails filling our inbox so that we can't receive or send any more messages until we've spent half an
hour deleting the junk.

Usually, though, the things that most deeply impact our
lives happen at the hands of people we know and trust.
Sometimes we are controlled by what someone says about us
behind our backs. Still in other circumstances, we are affected by something *unspoken*. A person who *should* have said
something did not take a stand and speak the truth.

This control over our lives is not always exercised by the
actions or words of individual people. Sometimes institutions, such as a school or workplace, big business, the government, or even the church can impact us. Because an institution did not carry out what it promised or because it
did not live up to what we thought it stood for, we can come
to mistrust all institutions like it.

Depending upon the general nature of our personality,
our lives can be controlled in one of two ways by the actions
of others. On the one hand, some of us tend to withdraw
from living in authentic community when we are hurt. At
best, we live the rest of our lives in a sort of pretend community, acting as if we trust and share life with other people
but constantly being apprehensive about truly participating.
At worst, we live the rest of our lives in isolation and mistrust of other people.

Others are more aggressive in seeking retaliation. We
find ways to get even—some person or institution has to pay
for what was done to us. Reparation for what was done or
said becomes foremost in our minds.

THE DOMINANT ECONOMY: HOLDING ON

As people act in ways that hurt, disappoint, or anger us, we become amazing bookkeepers—even if we can't balance our own checkbooks. We end up living by a very familiar economy of debt accumulation, and we hold on tightly to those tabs, sometimes even charging interest, until they are paid back.

Holding on to what other people say or do often has devastating and destructive effects upon our lives. The ongoing focus upon disappointment and hurt caused by another creates space in our lives for cynicism and bitterness to develop. As a result, we begin mistrusting even persons and institutions not involved in the immediate disappointment. Suspicion and negativity can begin to characterize our personality and keep us spiritually and emotionally stuck.

AN ALTERNATIVE ECONOMY: LETTING GO

The opposite of *holding on* is *letting go*. When life is truly experienced as a sheer gift, we come to celebrate that God has canceled the debt entirely. The price we could not pay, we no longer owe!

In turn, as other people or institutions owe us something, we enact the cancelation of their debts. The price they might or might not be able to pay, they no longer owe! This gift-driven life of *letting go* is often described in terms of forgiveness. At its heart, a life of forgiveness is a life that sets other people free from their debts. Even more, forgiveness miraculously loosens the imprisoning chains upon the one who can finally say, "Your debt is canceled!"

This alternative economy has its biblical roots in the Israelite year of jubilee. In Lev. 25, there is an odd stipulation that says that every 50 years, a trumpet must blow throughout the land as the people "proclaim liberty throughout the land to all its inhabitants" (v. 10). The ramifications of this celebration were profound. Any land that was sold due to the inability to pay off debts would be returned to the original owner. Anyone who became a slave because he or she was unable to pay off a debt would be released from servitude.

In this system, amassing IOUs from other people was not the most important thing because everyone knew that eventually those IOUs were good for nothing. In this system, accumulation of stuff at the expense of everyone else was useless, because all the stuff would eventually be returned in the year of jubilee.

This economy is so different from what we are used to that it almost sounds absurd. However, in the mind of God and in the mind of God's people, life was a gift. It was not traded in. It was not borrowed. It was not sold. It was a sheer gift. And where life is a gift, a strange economy exists—one that refuses to *hold on*, and in contrast, *lets go*.

Many people today believe that our Israelite ancestors never actually observed a jubilee, for obvious reasons. On the one hand, there is no record of its observance anywhere in the Old Testament, and the social and economic ramifications would have been massive even if it were put into practice a single time. On the other hand, just practically speaking, why would anyone with wealth and power want to practice jubilee? It makes no sense. If other people owe you, why let go of their debts?

But the prophet Isaiah envisioned a day in the future in which jubilee would be a reality. He spoke of it in these terms: "The spirit of the Lord GOD is upon me, because the Lord has anointed me; he has sent me to bring good news to the oppressed, to bind up the brokenhearted, to proclaim liberty to the captives, and release to the prisoners; to proclaim the year of the LORD's favor" (Isa. 61:1-2). Imagine wholeness for those whose lives are torn apart because of their enormous debts, liberty and release for those who sold themselves into servitude in order to pay what they owed. Indeed, this would be the time of favor—the season of grace—the year of jubilee!

The whole alternative vision of a debt-free world may

have eventually been forgotten if not for one significant voice—the voice of Jesus himself. Early in His ministry, Jesus made His way to the synagogue. There He opened up the scroll of the prophet Isaiah and began reading from it. He read the message of this alternative Kingdom—a Kingdom of good news to the debt-ridden, healing for the downtrodden, release for captives. He read the good news of the season of grace. Then after He rolled the scroll back up, put it back in its place, and sat down, He said, "Today this scripture has been fulfilled in your hearing" (Luke 4:21).

Jesus embodied just what this type of jubilee kingdom looked like. Sinners who had no power in themselves to enter the kingdom of God were admitted. Outcasts like lepers and tax collectors and prostitutes whose very lifestyles had so stacked up the IOUs that they could never pay back what they owed were forgiven and set free. Sick people who had no strength in themselves to be healed were healed, and demon-possessed people who were so deep into the mire of evil that they had no hope of coming back were released and freed and sent on their way whole again. People who did not deserve, could not pay, were in debt over their heads, were given a gift—a sheer, pure gift.

Jubilee is more than an event every 50 years. It is the ongoing, continual economy of the kingdom of God.

In relationship to our past actions, this means that we do not have to take out extra loans or think that somehow, someday we can do just enough for God and pay back all that He has done for us. That would be impossible! Instead, our debt is canceled.

Like the story of the prodigal son, our Father has already released the debts owed by His children! Before we ever turn around and decide to come back home, God has *let go* of all of the debts we owe. Imagine that! While we are still in the pigpen trying to figure out how we can set up a payment plan to fulfill our obligations from yesterday, the debts have already been released. While we are sitting around trying to come up with a way to become a production-oriented servant and pay back what we owe Him, God already has the robe and the crown and the fattened calf prepared. He's just waiting for us to *accept* His cancelation of our debts.

As He taught His followers how to pray, Jesus directly linked God's forgiveness of our debts to our forgiveness of each other's debts. In other words, this economy is not merely from God to us. It trickles down into the smallest recesses of our lives and affects every relationship of which we are a part. Thus, we are taught to ask God to "forgive us our debts, as we also have forgiven our debtors" (Matt. 6:12, NIV). We have *spiritualized* these words into sins or trespasses. However, the prayer literally reflects words of jubilee: debts and debtors—that which we owe God and that which people owe us.

Imagine the ramifications of this alternative economy in our relationships. Forgiveness is simply that which we grant—whether or not anyone asks for it. Forgiveness is the refusal to keep *holding on* and the decision to *let go* of all that a person or institution owes us. No doubt, letting go is setting the other person free so he or she can move on; however, it is likewise liberating us from the tight grip we have on the other person so we can finally move on as well.

SOME COMMON MISCONCEPTIONS

This act of *letting go* is most often described as forgiveness. Because the understanding of forgiveness is often filled with many mistaken notions, we can easily live our lives never really letting go. There are many misconceptions about forgiveness.

Misconception 1: Forgiveness Is Dependent upon the Other Person's Apology. Forgiveness is not related to the response of the person or institution that has wronged us. While it would certainly be welcomed in many situations, remorse or the admission of wrong by another person is not a requirement before we can or should forgive. Oftentimes, waiting for another person to apologize can become a justification for remaining where we are in life and not moving on into God's tomorrow.

Tragically, we can spend years of our lives waiting for an apology from someone and never receive it. In the end, we've lost out on the beauty of the gift of life while we were stuck waiting. Forgiveness is not a *reaction* to what someone else says or does. Rather, forgiveness is the *proactive* step of letting go of the accumulated debt of another person and moving forward.

Misconception 2: Based upon the Nature of the Wrong That Was Done, I Have the Right to Hold On. When it comes to the wounds that leave the deepest scars, it is easy to convince ourselves that the difficult nature of our particular circumstance justifies not letting go. We can even make the distinction between intentional and unintentional actions, deciding that the unintentional are forgivable but that intentional injuries are not.

A bandage approach that hides the wound and yet continues to secretly nurture it by repeatedly reliving the situation with playbacks of what was done to us allows the wound to fester and even become more grossly infected. Authentic healing of the wounds only begins to take place as we release our grip on what was done or what was said—no matter how severe the wound. As we let go, we finally move on.

Misconception 3: Forgiveness Is Saying "I'm Sorry." Perhaps one of the most common misconceptions about forgiveness is that it means apologizing in every situation. For whatever reason, we confuse *asking for* forgiveness with the act of forgiveness itself. No doubt, in many relationships where injury has been inflicted by both parties in the relationship, an apology may be called for. However, extending forgiveness is not based upon our admission of wrong any more than it is hearing the other person admit he or she was wrong. Forgiveness is simply releasing the hold we have on another person or institution, or perhaps better said, it is releasing ourselves from the hold he or she or it has on our lives.

When we are able to let go and move on, there is a much

greater freedom to express an apology when it is due. Being able to say "I'm sorry" for what we said or for what we did permits us to be released from the convicting sense that we should admit our wrong in a situation.

Misconception 4: Forgiveness Can Only Take Place When the Circumstances Are Appropriate. How many times in life can waiting for the right situation become the perfect excuse for doing nothing? More often than not, the appropriate circumstances never come along. As a result, we continue to hold the wrong that was done as it continually festers and reemerges in our lives and relationships.

The time for letting go is in the present so that we can genuinely move on into God's tomorrow as free people.

Misconception 5: Forgiveness Is Forgetting. Probably the most common misconception of forgiveness is that it is about *forgetting*. Have you ever *tried* to forget something? At least in my case, the more I try to forget something, the more it comes to my mind. Forgiveness is not a mental exercise of forgetting. It is not some type of amnesia that we give ourselves. Self-inflicted memory loss is an absurd idea!

Rather than a mental practice of forgetting, forgiveness is actually a physical exercise of letting go. Perhaps one of the greatest truths about letting go is that while we may still recall vividly in our memory what was done or said in the past, we are freed from its controlling power upon our lives in the present.

Misconception 6: Forgiveness Is a Form of "Deferred Payment." A final misconception concerning forgiveness is that it is a way of psychologically deferring payment for a wrong done to us . . . temporarily. Too often, this subtle form of *holding on* can take a very odd form. Rather than settling the score directly with the other person, we wait for a moment or situation that will show the other person just how wrong they really were. We may not even desire to encounter the person, but we continue to wait for a time in the future that will put that person in his or her place and finally get the last word. We say we've forgiven someone, but truthfully, we're keeping a card in our back pocket to pull out and play when it's most advantageous.

Obviously, this way of thinking is not forgiveness, for ultimately we continue to hold on to what was said or done to us. We're just delaying our retaliation. Much like those two-years-same-as- cash deals, we defer the payback for a lengthy period of time, but we still anticipate when that time of payback comes.

LETTING GO—AUTHENTICALLY

Perhaps no story in all of Scripture more vividly paints a picture of letting go than the story of Joseph's encounter with his brothers many years after they sold him into slavery and faked his death in a plot of jealousy. After all that was done to him, Joseph announces, "Do not be afraid! Am I in the place of God? Even though you intended to do harm to me, God intended it for good, in order to preserve a numerous people, as he is doing today. So have no fear; I myself will provide for you and your little ones" (Gen. 50:19-21).

Joseph refused to take revenge or settle the score at the one moment in his life when he finally had power over his brothers to do to them whatever he wished. Even though his brothers bowed in a posture of homage and said, "We'll be your slaves," Joseph refused to get even. How was he able to do this? What allowed him to authentically let go of the power they had over him?

Authentic forgiveness emerges from knowing who is, and who is not God. With Joseph's question to his brothers, he said a mouthful: "Am I in the place of God?" Recognizing that he ultimately did not have to play the role of God in his brothers' lives allowed Joseph to let go of any desire he might have had to overpower them or manipulate their lives.

Just as importantly as recognizing that he was not God, Joseph also recognized that those who attempted to manipulate and control his life were not God either. While the brothers intended to harm his life, they ultimately did not have the final say in Joseph's life. God always has the final say! No family member, no work colleague, no friend, no institution in the end is God. Certain people and even certain institutions may attempt to play God in other people's lives, but they are not God. Recognizing this reality allowed Joseph to let go of the self-deceived persons who thought they had control.

Recognizing who *is* God and who *is not* God is vital to authentic forgiveness.

Authentic forgiveness recognizes the creative power of God. It is a promise of Scripture. The God who brought light into darkness and peace into chaos can take whatever dark, chaotic situations come our way and work them together into life and light and peace and salvation. He is the Creator God, and He continues to create.

Joseph has no need to *hold on* to the chaos and brokenness that his brothers brought into his life. Why hold on to darkness when God brings light? Why clasp so tightly to the hurt and pain caused by others when God brings wholeness and restoration? Why settle for bandaged wounds when God brings deep healing? The capacity to *let go* and move on emerges from the recognition that God is the creative One who takes the ugliest canvases of life and makes them masterpieces.

Authentic forgiveness moves beyond blame games. As Joseph announced that what his brothers reckoned as evil, God reckoned as good, the word "reckon" is not a word of causation. Joseph was *not* saying that God caused these terrible situations in his life. Rather, the word comes from the world of accountants whose task was to add up all the numbers and tally the results. What Joseph was saying is that once all the tallying of his life was over, Joseph's brothers saw the sum in the negative column: *evil.* On the other hand, in God's mathematical system, even including the negative numbers of Joseph's life, the final sum ended up in the positive column: *for the good.* Ultimately this sum was the result of God's creative ability to take the chaos and bring good out of it.

Similarly, Joseph did not point a finger at evil forces and powers, whether spiritual or human, and describe them as the source of his past difficulties. It would have been easy for Joseph to describe his victimization at the hands of his brothers or the hands of Potiphar's wife, or even the hands of Pharaoh. However, Joseph refused to play the blame game.

Blaming is one of the most paralyzing and debilitating exercises into which we can get ourselves. Was it something we did to bring this on ourselves? Is God punishing us, or perhaps is He putting us through a difficult time to refine us and make us better persons? Is Satan attacking us because he knows we are weak, or on the other hand is he attacking us because he knows we are too strong? Was the situation the result of a weak government? A bad person? A corrupt business? A dysfunctional family? A misguided church?

As long as finding a target for blame is our fixation, the capacity to let go and move on is restricted. On the other hand, when we can move our gaze from the events of yesterday, look in our hand at today, and let go of everything else we are holding so tightly, we step toward God's hope-filled future.

Authentic forgiveness lets go and moves on with life. In the end, the story of Joseph is a story of release. Joseph releases his brothers from whatever debts they owe. Although they offer themselves as slaves, he refuses the payment of their IOUs. His ability to *let go* allowed him to move on—providing for his family, giving them words of reassurance, and living at peace.

In contrast to the popular economy of holding on, the economy of living life as God's sheer gift is one of letting go—truly *letting go*—and getting on with life. The only way to move on is to crumple up the debts, tear them apart, and allow them to blow away in the wind. With that act of letting go, we can move on and share this beautiful, pure gift of life in authentic community with other people.

THE STRANGEST FORGIVENESS

There is a strange forgiveness that really should be mentioned. There are times in life we might come to hold God himself responsible. When the sun is shining and the sky is blue, matters such as God's involvement in life's crises is an interesting theoretical matter. However, when the crises of life come to us firsthand, it is no longer an interesting theory to debate, but it often is a struggling matter of life and death, trust and doubt, peace and anxiety.

The questions are all familiar. *Where was God when . . . If God, then why . . . Why didn't God intervene? I did everything the Bible says, but God did not . . . I thought I was following God's will, and then . . .*

On the front end, we should not be afraid to admit that we ask these questions. They are the questions with which God's people have struggled throughout all time. Often, these questions are not as much the questions of doubt as they are questions of trusting people who are seeking some type of understanding and consolation from the God whom they love and in whom they have great trust.

Perhaps there are answers to some of these questions. Nevertheless, we want God in some form or fashion to explain himself. We want Him to give us an answer. We might even long to hear Him say, "I'm sorry."

God has already shown up with His answer. He wrapped himself up in flesh and participated in this life with all of its unanswered questions with us. Not only did He come 2,000 years ago, but He is the God who continues coming. He steps into life's unanswered questions with us. He even participates in the most desperate cry that we human beings can utter: "My God! My God! Why have you forsaken me?" As odd as it sounds, He is with us in the times when we sense God-forsakenness the deepest. He cries out with us.

How do we respond to the God who suffers with us and weeps with us and cries out in desperation with us and even dies with us? Ultimately, we *let go* of that paralyzing sense that "God owes me." We *let go* of the IOU that we have even written up for God . . . and with God walking alongside us, we move on into His bright and new tomorrow.

9

Becoming Hope-Filled Lovers

I admittedly fulfill the stereotype of a bachelor by making frequent stops at the grocery store just to make sure I can use the seven items or less line. It makes no sense, truthfully. The express line is always the longest. But somehow I have convinced myself that it's still faster to use this line several times a week than to plan a real grocery list and stand in a full-order line once each week.

So recently, I stopped at the store, grabbed my few items, and headed for the express line. I quickly recognized I was in a bad situation. As I looked ahead, it was obvious that the cashier was either new or having a really bad day. The line was moving slower than ever. All three people ahead of me found mistakes on their receipts that had to be corrected. I became increasingly frustrated with the whole situation.

All three customers ahead of me gave her a piece of his or her mind, and I began working up my own little speech. I didn't plan to speak *that* harshly, but since I had waited for 10 minutes now, I felt justified in saying something.

I finally reached her register. I took my seven items out of the basket and put them on the counter. I looked up, ready to deliver my speech, and noticed that she was wearing a little badge that said something like Hello, my name is . . . Scribbled underneath was her name, *Mary*. I imagined it would be good to start my reprimand with her name, so I looked at her and said "Hello, Mary."

Before I could get anything else out, tears began to flow down her cheeks. I thought, "Wow! I haven't even started; wait until she hears the rest of it!"

She looked at me and through tears that were so human, so real, she softly said, "Thank you." Her response startled me, so I replied, "Thank you for what?"

She explained how she had worked a double shift the day before. When she arrived home at about 11 P.M., she found a note left by her husband. The note simply stated that he could no longer live up to what she and their three children demanded of him and he needed time off for a few weeks to find himself again. Through her tears, she explained to me, "I don't know what I'm going to do. I can't support myself and my three kids on this job. All I've been thinking today is how I'm going to survive—how my kids and I can make it. I've been making mistakes all day. Nobody understands; nobody wants to understand. People assume I'm just the *slow cashier who doesn't know what she's doing*. Anyway . . . thanks . . . that was the first time I've heard my name all day. It reminded me that I really am more than a mommy, more than a wife, more than a slow cashier. I'm Mary."

By now, I felt about two inches tall. My speech evaporated. As tears swelled up in my own eyes, I realized just how quick I am to see people for their performance and productivity. Some are strong, acceptable, indispensable producers; others are weak, unacceptable, and dispensable.

I was now holding up the very line that had earlier led to my own frustration, but I accidentally realized a little more about what it means to partner with God in looking beyond labels.

Just as God's gift of life to us is an ongoing, continual gift, extending life to others becomes an uninterrupted and consistent way of *being* in our world that affects our way of living in even the tiniest corners of our lives. We become bearers of God's gift of life. We become instruments of God's grace in the lives of our closest friends and family members as well as casual acquaintances and even strangers. Beyond the periodic momentous events of service, we extend life to others through our everyday living. Our routine, commonplace lives at home, at school, at the workplace, and in the community become the vessels through which God can breathe breath into lifelessness, announce forgiveness where there is debt, and speak light into situations of darkness.

JESUS—THE ULTIMATE HOPE-FILLED LOVER

The greatest model we have for extending life is found in the ministry of Jesus himself. The pulse of His ministry was what might best be described as hope-filled love. Extending His pure gift of life to others ultimately provided them more than a religious drug that sedated them for a while and allowed them to cope with life. It was more than a single meal that filled their hunger for a day. It was more than bandages to hide the wounds and bruises of life.

He offered them more.

He offered transformation, a brand-new life. While He loved people where they were, He envisioned life with hope that God's life-changing grace was so real and so active that no life was incapable of transformation. All lives could indeed grow and develop and be transformed.

Jesus offered reconciliation and adoption into a family to outcasts who lived all of their lives on the fringes of society. He offered light and sound and mobility to people who had never been able to see or hear or walk. He offered resurrection and new life to the spiritually and physically dead.

In the same way, for us, extending the gift of life to others is ultimately participating with Jesus Christ in extending hope into the lives of our world. It is having an optimism that springs forth from God's transforming, life-changing grace.

While giving relief is of great significance, the hope that we extend is more than relief. While providing means to cope with life situations is valuable, we offer more than the capacity to cope.

We are called to join Christ as hope-filled lovers who extend the optimism of promise. The love of God has always been filled with promise—promise to a people in exile that God will make a way back home even when it seems impossible; promise to people undergoing persecution and affliction that God will be with them in a lions' den or a fiery furnace; promise to prostitutes and tax collectors that they have a place at His table.

The prophet Jeremiah was very well aware of the hope-filled love of God. Writing a letter to persons whose dreams were shattered and who were experiencing the grief of exile, Jeremiah declares, "I know the plans I have for you, says the LORD, plans for your welfare and not for harm, to give you *a future with hope*" (Jer. 29:11, emphasis added). These plans of God are not about prosperous jobs, big houses, or successful careers. His plans are for wholeness in our lives. He holds the future wide open with this hope. This is the hope-filled love of God in which we participate. This is the life-giving love of God that we share with friends, family, colleagues, neighbors, and even strangers: *a future with hope.*

Paul describes hope-filled love in this way: "It bears all things, believes all things, hopes all things, endures all things. Love never ends" (1 Cor. 13:7-8). It is tenacious, steadfast, and persistent. This hope-filled love always knows that the transforming grace of God goes deeper, higher, and wider than any brokenness, pain, or sin. It does not have strings attached that say, "I will love you *if*" or "I will love you *when*" Nor does it say, "I will love you because of what you can become." It simply says, "I love you," and then it dares to step into the life of another and share life with that other person, believing so strongly that the life-giving

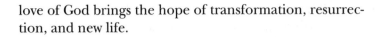

love of God brings the hope of transformation, resurrection, and new life.

OBSTACLES TO BECOMING HOPE-FILLED LOVERS

Why are we often more comfortable with putting a few dollars in an envelope and sending it to an important relief effort than with stepping into the life of someone we know very well and holding out hope in the nighttime of his or her life? Why is it easier for us to take a week's vacation and help construct a church thousands of miles away from our home than it is to take a moment with the neighbor next door and share hope-filled love?

To be honest, during the normal days of our lives, we're just too busy and too focused on what must be done before the day is over. At work, there are tasks to complete. At the gas station, we want to get in and out as quickly as possible. Even at church, we get so caught up in teaching the class or singing in the choir or cooking the meal that we are as task-driven there as during the rest of the week. Finally, when we get home, pick up the mail, open and close the garage door, and check our messages, who has the energy to look toward our next-door neighbors?

In certain pain-filled situations, all we can honestly see is the hopelessness. Looking at the situation realistically and honestly, it is just too bleak to imagine any type of hope-filled alternative. It is extremely difficult to hold out hope to another person when we have lost all sense of optimism ourselves.

While we seldom recognize it, one of the greatest obstacles to stepping into the lives of other people and sharing hope-filled love with those who are experiencing brokenness is the required face-to-face confrontation with our own humanness and mortality. Sharing intimately in the wounds and brokenness and grief of other people reminds us that we face the same realities. We see our own human frailty. It is just much easier to avoid face-to-face encounters with the hurts of other people so that we maintain a safe distance from their physical, relational, and emotional brokenness.

BECOMING HOPE-FILLED LOVERS

The life that God gives us is filled with an optimism that emerges from His faithful life-giving and life-transforming presence. He loves too deeply to provide simple bandages that conceal wounds. He hopes too fiercely to shut the door to tomorrow and lock it. This Divine Lover invites us to participate in His life-giving gift of hope-filled love in the lives and daily affairs of colleagues, friends, family members, and strangers.

1. Hope-filled Lovers Know the Source of Hope. In the attempt to extend hope to other people, we can easily become trapped in a reality that believes our actions and words are the ultimate source of hope. We need to be reminded from time to time that God is the real Source of hope, not us.

We may love to feel needed but none of us has a large Superman "S" imprinted on his or her chest. It's easy for caring people to get caught up in believing they are miracleworkers who can solve problems, but we simply do not possess the capacity to *fix* all of the difficulties of people and situations around us. Unfortunately, out of the simple desire to extend hope and love, we can lose focus and forget who we are. We are means of God's grace; we are extenders of the gift of life. But we point beyond ourselves to the source of this gift.

Hope-filled lovers also know they cannot control people. When this is forgotten, we may try to create situations in which a person *needs* our help or assistance. As a result, relationships that began out of a deep desire to love and extend hope can become suffocating, life-killing relationships of manipulation and control all under the guise of care. Our identity can end up becoming grounded in just how much we are needed by someone else. Acts of compassion can become acts of control, and gifts of love can become gifts of manipulation. In the end, the once hope-filled lover again becomes an achievement-driven, accomplishment-oriented performer. In an odd way, it's like basing our identity on our ability to produce in the life of another person. Grace is gone, and performance reemerges.

Ultimately, hope-filled lovers know their own limitations. They know they are human and not divine. They know they cannot solve all of the world's problems or fix everybody's situation. They dare to take their hands off the control of other people's lives by creating situations where they *must* be present. They point away from dependency upon themselves and toward dependency upon the only Source of true hope—God.

2. Hope-filled Lovers See People as People. Once we truly discover that our identity is based on being recipients of life purely because of God's love for us and not on being producers, we start seeing others as more than machines. Our focus moves from asking, "What have they done for me lately?" to seeing them as people who laugh and love and weep and dream.

The life of Abraham and Sarah is one of the most beautiful stories in the Bible that portrays the power of seeing people as people. God's promise to give them a child brought a response of disbelieving laughter. It sounded so ridiculous that they took matters into their own hands and brought Hagar, their maidservant, into the story.

It actually was the custom, even the law, that when a wife could not bear a child, the maidservant of the family would act as a surrogate so the couple could have descendants. In other words, seeing their own weaknesses and inabilities, Abraham and Sarah were following the customary practice of their day.

The manner in which Abraham and Sarah refer to Hagar in Gen. 16 and 21 is fascinating. They never refer to Hagar by her personal name. They speak of her through labels —labels that particularly describe her in terms of what she *does* rather than in terms of who she *is*. She is the *maidservant*, but for Abraham and Sarah she is not *Hagar*.

The story doesn't end there. As the *maidservant* finds herself stripped of her personhood and alone in the wilderness, a fourth character shows up. Do you notice how God always seems to show up in the wilderness experiences of life? The first word He speaks is remarkable. To the nameless maidservant who was merely an object to people of promise, God's first word is "Hagar." To the one whose personhood was replaced by the job she could do, God gave her back her name. To the one who was viewed by others as no more than an object that could be used for their own hope-filled lives, God restores hope by seeing her simply for who she was—Hagar!

Before the encounter in the wilderness ends, the maid who was given back her name is permitted to give God a name. She calls Him El Roi—God sees me! And then she names her son Ishmael—God hears! God sees me; God hears. What amazing, hope-filled words she speaks when God shows up and simply sees her as an individual—Hagar.

Hope-filled lovers dare to look beyond the labels and see people as real people to whom God is calling. Hope-filled lovers participate with God in looking beyond the labels and restoring people's names.

Sometimes these people who become labels are those closest to us. Even people with whom we share life's most intimate moments can be viewed more by what they do or don't do, how well they do or do not perform, what they can or can't accomplish, more than by who they are. It's easy to forget that our closest friend, roommate, parent, sibling, or child is a human being with real feelings and thoughts and fears and dreams.

Other times, the people who are reduced to labels are the anonymous strangers in our lives—the attendant at the service station, the person who works on another floor, or the next-door neighbor we rarely see. We see them but never notice them; we hear them but never listen to them.

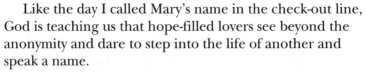

Like the day I called Mary's name in the check-out line, God is teaching us that hope-filled lovers see beyond the anonymity and dare to step into the life of another and speak a name.

3. *Hope-filled Lovers Exercise the Gift of Presence.* During my sophomore year in college, my father, a healthy, stout 50-year-old preacher, came down with the flu over Christmas break. He showed no improvement after a week and finally went to the hospital for tests. By that evening, my mother and two older brothers returned home with the news. With my youngest brother in her lap, my mother began to explain, "Daddy has been diagnosed with acute leukemia."

For the next week, a million thoughts, questions, and uncertainties filled my mind. Why was this happening? How could I go back to school and pretend like life was moving ahead? But both of my parents convinced me that dropping out of college was not an option, so I returned to school for the spring semester.

With many rounds of chemotherapy and the gracious touch of God, by late spring, my dad was in remission. He had a relatively good summer and we shared many laughs together. Ordinarily missed moments of life were fully embraced and celebrated by the family. Simply sitting under a tree and eating newly ripened apples took on meaning. Watching a rabbit race across the lawn brought joy like it did when we were young children. We waited for everyone to show up for meals instead of racing through so we could get to our next appointment. It's amazing how we can finally learn what it means to live when confronted with the reality of death.

I had been back to college for a couple weeks the next school year when the phone in my dormitory room rang. My mom was on the other end. The news was not good. The cancer cells had returned, and this time they were back with a vengeance. Each weekend for the next six months, I made the three-hour trip to the hospital. During that time, I went through every spiritual exercise imaginable: praying intensively several times daily, regularly fasting meals, mentally concentrating on envisioning my dad healthy and whole again. You name it, I probably did it.

The month of March rolled around. I was home for the weekend, speaking at a youth service in a local church. On the way back home late one evening, I passed by the hospital and noticed my mother's car was still in the parking lot. From the street I could tell that the light in my father's hospital room was on. I quickly parked the car and ran up to the room. He had slipped into a coma from the time I left him a couple of hours earlier. My family gathered around his bedside and within hours, I watched my father gasp for his last breath.

I so believed that God was going to intervene and do something, I kept watching, knowing that he would begin to breathe again. But he didn't. We were eventually escorted out of the room by the hospital staff.

Two days later, I stood at the head of the casket of the man whom I had loved and admired more than any person on earth. He was my mentor, my hero, my model. I just could not understand it. *Why? How? What if?*

Many well-meaning people moved around the casket to where I was standing and offered consolation statements like, "He really has been healed now" and "God is going to make you such a strong young man out of this" and "We'll never know why, but God has a reason for everything" and "Even if he could come back now, he wouldn't want to." I have to admit, it all left me numb. It was as if I were standing in a hot, dry desert longing for a sip of water and many were giving me cups and glasses and jars . . . but they were empty. I was thirsty! I just needed a small sip of hope.

Nobody seemed to know who he was or how he knew of the death. He was a middle-aged man who stepped forward and looked down at the casket. He then made his way over to where I was standing. In silence, he looked at me with tears. He gazed into my eyes and somehow penetrated my soul as he simply said, "I was 20 when my dad died." He embraced me and we wept.

Finally, the rain fell on my wilderness journey. I got my first taste of hope. The dryness was touched not with deep answers or sophisticated explanations or fancy, well-articulated words. The dryness was touched with the sheer presence of this man. It wasn't his words. He was with me. He suffered with me. He wept with me. He participated with me. And his simple presence—a presence that dared to share and participate in my life—brought hope.

Hope-filled lovers know the significance of presence. They know the value of a God who did not come with deep explanations or well-articulated answers. He simply came. He wrapped himself up in the flesh of a crying baby and wept when we wept and cried out in pain as He was dying. He truly lived *with* us. There was something about His presence, Him simply being *with us* in every stage of life that made all the difference in the world.

In the same way, hope-filled lovers share life with other people *wherever* they are and *just as* they are. They do not demand that people change first. Hope-filled love does not have strings attached. It does not place time limitations on the hope. It endures and perseveres and holds on and never gives up. It keeps dreaming; it continues to hope. Hope-filled lovers dare to believe that simply by sharing life with another, hope is extended.

4. Hope-filled Lovers Move Beyond the Past and See Beyond the Present. In extending the gift of hope-filled life to us, God does not simply cover His eyes to conceal the realities that we face. He brings authentic change and healing. The gift of life that He extends is filled with the hope of transformation. God really does take us from where we are and provide us with the hope of healing, wholeness, forgiveness, and new life! God never looks at the past and says, "I give up!" He never looks at the present and says, "Impossible!" He is never intimidated or overcome with sealed tombs; He is always moving life toward resurrection. He holds tomorrow wide open and invites us to continue on with the journey.

As hope-filled lovers, we dare to look beyond the sin and

brokenness of a person's past. Likewise, we dare to look beyond the apparent impossibilities of today and imagine a future of new life and possibilities. While we do not ignore the
realities of yesterday or cover up the situations of today,
hope-filled lovers always seek to take the hand of another
from yesterday's darkness and today's shadows and move on
into God's life-changing, transforming journey that takes us
into a tomorrow of open-ended possibilities.

5. ***Hope-filled Lovers Particularly Look Out for Persons Who
Are Easily Missed or Ignored.*** The prophets of Israel regularly
challenged God's people to be alert to those persons among
them who were easily ignored, people like social outcasts
and the sick, children and widows, the physically and social-
ly weak. Jesus even went so far as to say that feeding the
hungry, clothing the naked, visiting the imprisoned, and
taking care of the sick was the same as carrying out those
very acts toward Him (Matt. 25:35-40).

Hope-filled lovers keep their eyes open to the least
among us. They share an empathizing sensitivity with people who have no one else holding out hope and extending
the indescribable gift of life.

We really don't have to look too hard to discover people
in these situations. They are often right in front of our eyes,
falling through the cracks of our communities, families,
workplaces, and churches.

Maybe it's a child who desperately needs a mentor in life
while his parent is busy making ends meet. Hope-filled love
might spend a little time just throwing a ball, teaching a
musical instrument, or training in computers. Or maybe it
reaches the teenager who needs an adult figure to listen pa-
tiently without pointing an accusing finger.

Perhaps hope is most needed for the family member
who needs the simple assurance, through both words and
actions, that she is indeed an integral part of the family unit
and is not the family outcast and no matter what she does
or where she goes, she will always belong to the family.

Or maybe a person in the office needs to know that he is

more than a human machine carrying out the menial tasks no one else wants to do.

Hope-filled love at church might open our hearts to the individual who rebelled and turned away from faith and is now fearful of the judgment from other members of the church.

Perhaps we need to extend hope-filled life by visiting the nursing home resident whose closest relative lives hundreds of miles away.

We might discover opportunities to share hope-filled love to the nameless uninsured individual who has mounting medical bills or the prisoner who is paying for the crime but needs someone to believe he is still redeemable, or the impoverished woman who needs someone to offer her a job.

The list could go on and on, but throughout the little corner of the world in which we find ourselves, women and men and adolescents and children wait to hear, to see, to taste, and to touch the good news that the door to tomorrow does indeed remain unlocked and open. They wait to have hope-filled love extended and poured out into their lives. We don't have to look very far!

A PRAYER FOR THE HOPE-FILLED JOURNEY

Because a tomb that was sealed shut was not the final word, hope-filled lovers dare to believe that the most impossible dead-ends of sin or brokenness or failure or despair are never final for any human being. They dare to persist in the optimism of divine grace that does not conceal or masquerade but instead transforms, changes, and breathes new life! Hope-filled lovers see other people as real, live human beings rather than as objects that stand in the way to a predetermined goal or objects that can be used and manipulated to get to those predetermined goals. They know the life-changing significance of simple presence—*being* even before doing or saying.

The hope-filled lover knows the ultimate source of authentic hope—the gift-giving, life-breathing God of all creation! Therefore, hope-filled life begins with a posture of openness to this God—opening our lives to His grace and peace, love and mercy. This openness seeks every opportunity to extend hope to family and strangers, colleagues and neighbors. As we open our own lives to this life-giving, hope-filled God, we become vessels of His very life and hope.

Perhaps the 13th-century prayer of Francis of Assisi best articulates the prayer of openness—the prayer that opens our lives to becoming extensions of grace and peace, hope and life:

> *Lord, make me an instrument of Thy peace;*
> *Where there is hatred, let me sow love;*
> *Where there is injury, pardon;*
> *Where there is doubt, faith;*
> *Where there is despair, hope;*
> *Where there is darkness, light;*
> *And where there is sadness, joy.*
>
> *O Divine Master,*
> *Grant that I may not so much seek to be consoled as to console;*
> *To be understood, as to understand;*
> *To be loved, as to love;*
> *For it is in giving that we receive,*
> *It is in pardoning that we are pardoned,*
> *And it is in dying that we are born to eternal life.*
> *Amen.*

CONCLUSION:
FINDING YOUR RHYTHM IN A PERFORMANCE-DRIVEN WORLD

The music of life is playing! However, there are so many other sounds—conversations about yesterday, plans for tomorrow, and a whole lot of dirty tables to clean today. While we're working faster, longer, and harder for a big tip at this table and a smile of approval from that table, the music of life continues to play. Might we dare to participate in the rhythm? In our performance-driven world where life has been based upon productivity and accomplishment since we were children, can we hear the music?

The failures of yesterday, the pressing deadlines of today, and the dreams for tomorrow can drown out the music. What if we paused just a little longer to listen to the music? What if we didn't rush around so quickly to squeeze in one more thing, but instead stopped for just a moment to gaze at the spectacular view? We might just crawl out of our seats, come to the floor, hear the music, find our rhythm . . . and who knows . . . maybe start participating in the childlike dance of life.

With arms extended and hands open, we reach up and graciously receive God's good gift of life. We are so vulnerable when we take that posture of reception. We've just gotten so used to always being the giver, the producer, the performance-driven child, teenager, employee, friend, parent, and churchgoer. All we can do is unwrap the gift, see it for what it is, and exclaim: "Thank You! Thank You," not because this gift looks just like we wanted it to look, or because all of the pieces now fit, but "thank You" for life—the pure and simple gift of life. "Thank You!" Knowing that this gift is not a commodity to trade in for something else, we now simply put it to use . . . by *living!*

With this most remarkable gift now held in our hands, we bring our arms inward to our heart, and we embrace this gift. We embrace the whole of life—the journey—every season along the way. We embrace the peace of knowing that this gift is indeed a dynamic gift; it is not static. It grows; it changes. Truly, seasons come, and seasons go. But this gift is not confined to one season; it is the fullness of all of life's seasons. Indeed, this journey consists of the mountain peaks as well as the valleys and a whole lot of flat roads.

Along the way, the *moments* of this life-journey are inhaled—moments that in the mad rush can so easily be missed. We see the sights, hear the sounds, smell the aromas, taste the flavors, and are touched by the feelings of this gift of life. All along the way, we pause—we *stop*—we embrace the Sabbath moments of life just to join hands and hearts and minds with God and look at this good gift of life that He has given us and exclaim in unison with Him, "It is very good!"

Knowing that holding on to life only leads to suffocation and staleness, we proceed to move from the posture of embrace to the posture of relinquishment as we extend the gift of life to the little corner of the world in which we find ourselves. With our arms and hands wide open, we keep the lights on in our lives. We keep the vacancy sign lit. We experience the joy of knowing that we belong to something bigger than ourselves; we share life with other human beings who also laugh and cry and dream and fail and hope. With arms outstretched and our lives wide open, we release the tight-fisted clutch of holding on to what others owe us. We stop waiting for compensation for what was previously said or done to us. We let go of the debts; we release the IOUs; we relinquish the skepticism and the cynicism that prohibits us from loving and trusting other people. There, in the release, we discover the freedom to live with others in genuine community.

With our God-given gift of life open to others, we become conduits of the hope-filled love that has been released into our own lives. We dare to see life in lifelessness, wholeness in brokenness, and hope in hopelessness. As we become hope-filled lovers, we see other people as more than obstacles or means to our own ends. We see them as people. We step into the lives of others and dare to believe that hope-filled love is extended through simply being there.

As our hands are extended in relinquishing this gift of life to others, we discover that we are once again in the very posture to receive life. So, trusting that the One who gave us life in the first place will continue to give us life, we listen to the music, discover the rhythm once more, and keep participating in the dance of God's good gift called life!

Discovering the rhythm of this gift and participating in the dance of life means that work and production take on an entirely different meaning. Rather than productivity being the source of our lives, the work we do and the accomplishments that emerge are simply the fruit of life that is received, embraced, and relinquished. Rather than our identities being grounded in the work we do and the accomplishments we make, our identities are grounded in grace—gift! Rather than our lives being defined by achievements and accomplishments, they are defined by the central recognition that life itself is a gift. We are gifted, graced, and blessed children of the divine Giver of life! Life is now viewed not as the prize that is won through our own productivity and then held on to for dear life, but it is now viewed as the gift to be shared with others!

With the trust of a child who has not yet been told the rules of the game for winning the prize, we receive the gift without imagining what strings might be attached. Like that child, we breathlessly and wondrously take that gift into our hands and open it and celebrate it, trusting that this gift is indeed a sheer, pure, uncomplicated gift. Impossible? Maybe so . . . in an accomplishment-oriented, achievement-based, performance-driven world. But with God, all things are possible! Landless nomads receive land, barren women give birth, deserts become gardens, people in exile return home. With God, human productivity does not bring life; the Giver of life brings life. With God all things are possible! Even camels can travel through the eye of a needle—even those of us who are rich in all of our productivity, wealthy in our accomplishments, and affluent in our achievements can experience the impossible.

"Oh, for grace to trust Him more . . ." Oh, for grace, to hear the music, to discover the rhythm, to join the dance of life!

The music is playing . . . the stage is set . . . the gift is yours! Remember—arms out, hands open: receive the gift of life. Arms in, hands close to the heart: embrace the gift of life. Arms back out, hands reopened: relinquish the gift of life. The gift of life—it's yours! Join the dance.